BLEND — 1: BACKGROUND AND DEVELOPMENTS

B SHACKEL AND D J PULLINGER

Library and Information Research Report 29

ABSTRACT

The report describes a four-year experimental programme jointly organised by two universities and called the Birmingham and Loughborough Electronic Network Development (BLEND). The aims are to assess the cost, efficiency and subjective impact of an electronic communication system, and to explore and evaluate alternative forms of user communication through an electronic journal and information network.

Using a host computer at the University of Birmingham, a community of about 50 scientists (Loughborough Information Network Community — LINC) was connected through the public telephone network to explore various types of communication including journals, newsletters, annotated abstracts, workshop conferences, co-operative authorship, etc. Following this start in 1981, five other communities have been using the system for these various types of electronic communication. Included in this report is a description of the first three years of the LINC and the development of the following on-line journals during this period:- a refereed papers journal (two numbers so far), a thriving poster papers journal, an exploratory journal of software reviews and a new journal with bibliographic references, abstracts and the possibility of reader annotation. Using the tele-conferencing software on which the system is based, there have been two successful on-line conferences and standard messaging is always well used.

Throughout the project relevant data are being gathered to enable the assessment of system and user performance, cost, usefulness and acceptability. These include several longitudinal studies which are due to be completed later in 1984, and those such as the six- and 35-month telephone surveys of the LINC. These last, fully described in the report, have contributed to the many enhancements made to the software.

ISBN 0 7123 3042 9
ISSN   0263 1709

Typeset and printed in Great Britain by
Quorn Selective Repro Ltd.

CONTENTS

LIST OF FIGURES

Note: All figures, diagrams and tables have been placed in a single
       numbering system and labelled 'Figures' to facilitate easy
       access.

FOREWORD

Costs escalating, journal circulation dropping, technology beckoning and indicating new possibilities — no wonder some pundits anticipate the paperless society. Electronic books, electronic newspapers and electronic journals are all discussed but what really are the possibilities? We need to look behind the glossy screen to how people live and work, how changes affect their lives. We need to be sure that electronic journals are not only technologically feasible but also commercially viable and humanly acceptable.

ACKNOWLEDGEMENTS

The research was funded by the British Library Research and Development Department and was carried out by the HUSAT Research Group, Department of Human Sciences, Loughborough University of Technology, in close collaboration with the Centre for Computing and Computer Studies, University of Birmingham.

In addition to the main authors, the following persons at Loughborough and Birmingham have contributed directly to the research presented in this report:

University of Birmingham:	Dr. W.P. Dodd
	Mr. T.I. Maude
Loughborough University of Technology:	Mrs. W. Olphert
	Miss K. Howey

There has been much help and encouragement from Professor P. Jarrett, University of Birmingham. The British Library staff have been considered an integral part of the Project Management Team and it is a pleasure to record our appreciation of the help given by them. The Advisory Committee for the Research and Development Department (ACORDD) and the New Technology Group have also given invaluable guidance upon occasions and supported fully the work undertaken.

We are also grateful for the co-operation and support of all the Loughborough Information Network Community (LINC) members without whom the project could not have been successfully operated and without whose helpfulness the data could not have been gathered.

In such a large experimental programme there are many to whom we are indebted and we hereby acknowledge any assistance given. In particular, Mrs. Sherry Herbert and then Mrs. Wendy Buckland, as secretaries to the research team at Loughborough, have cheerfully entered papers into the BLEND system and helped prepare all the papers and HUSAT memos which form the basis for this report.

PROJECT AIMS

The aims of the programme are to explore and evaluate forms of user communication through an 'electronic journal' and information network, and to assess the cost, efficiency and subjective impact of such a system.

To fulfil these aims a research programme was developed and organised jointly between the University of Birmingham and Loughborough University of Technology under the directorship of Professor Brian Shackel, hence the Birmingham and Loughborough Electronic Network Development, BLEND. The project team at Birmingham is responsible for operating and developing the system software, and that at Loughborough for developing communities and new uses, training and monitoring users and assessing the results.

The approach proposed and adopted aimed to be experimental rather than merely exploratory. Although the programme was started by getting an acceptable system into operation, the important part thereafter was to experiment with alternative methods and evaluate them properly (i.e. by valid and reliable test procedures with adequate numbers of users).

SCOPE OF THE REPORT

From the moment of its announcement in September 1980, this experimental programme has generated widespread interest amongst all those engaged in the scholarly publishing process, including editors, referees, publishers, information bureaux and libraries.

The research team was encouraged to disseminate widely the progress and findings of the experimental programme. Thus papers have appeared, or are about to appear, in the following journals and bulletins:

> *Aslib Proceedings*
> *Behaviour and Information Technology*
> *Bulletin of the Association of Learned and*
>   *Professional Society Publishers*
> *Communication Technology Impact*
> *Computer Compacts*
> *Computer Journal*
> *Data Processing*
> *Electronic Publishing Review*
> *Ergonomics*
> *International Journal of Man-Machine Studies*
> *IUCC Bulletin*
> *Journal of Librarianship*
> *Journal of the American Society for Information Science*

A full list of such publications may be found in Appendix 2; naturally other authors from the project team have been connected with some of these papers. Also two series of public seminars have been held and there have been many presentations at conferences, which are listed in Appendix 3.

This report on the background and history of the BLEND experimental programme is partly based on previously published papers and covers the origins of the experimental project, the establishing of the first community using the BLEND system and a description of the work of the first three years. Most of the quantitative research data are to be based on longitudinal comparisons over a $3\frac{1}{2}$ year period and will be presented in the final reports.

Thus, there is presented here in Part 1 of the Final Report a history of the initial stages, a description of enhancing the NOTEPAD software for the BLEND system, a discussion of various journal and organisational issues and a review of the LINC's first three years.

1 BACKGROUND AND HISTORY OF THE PROJECT

1.1 What is Computer Teleconferencing?

Computer teleconferencing is a way of conducting communication among groups or networks of people or organisations. It uses computers and computer terminals to provide (at the present time) a written form of discussion among a group of people, and has been described as halfway between a normal face-to-face conference and a very rapidly published newsletter (Palme, 1981).

To participate in a computer teleconference, the members of a group type their conference messages or contributions into a computer terminal which then transmits the textual material to the host computer. Each such message may contain text in any language which the author wants to put there. There are two kinds of messages: the first, called a *Note* or *Message,* is a private message from one user to another named user. The second kind, called a conference *Entry*, is stored sequentially according to time of origin in one of the conference areas known in the NOTEPAD and COM computer conferencing software suites as *Activities.* A number of users are named as members of a particular conference, i.e. an Activity. Each member would normally read all that is written in the Activity and might write Entries which are automatically available to all the other members of that Activity.

Instead of a face-to-face meeting in which only one person can talk at one time and all must be present at the same time in the same place, the use of the computer in this way means that individuals can call up the host computer and receive the text of conferences and messages at a pace, time and place of their own choosing. The users could all be making Entries and using the computer teleconferencing simultaneously, in locations spread throughout the world, or the sending and receiving of Notes and Entries could occur minutes, hours, days or even weeks and months apart.

The computer remembers which Notes and Entries each user has already had the opportunity of seeing. When users connect into the system, they are informed about and able to see all new Entries in each conference (Activity) of which they are a member, and they automatically receive all Notes addressed to them individually. They can then directly write Entries or Notes which will immediately be stored in the database. A typical user might connect to the system once or twice a week at personally convenient times, receive news, new Entries, etc., and write any comments or messages into the system. In this sense the system is similar to a very rapidly published newsletter.

The following diagram (Figure 1) illustrates that computer conferencing can cover a wide range of types of communication which are essentially new, allowing many people to communicate in a short space of time via the written word and providing a permanent record of so doing.

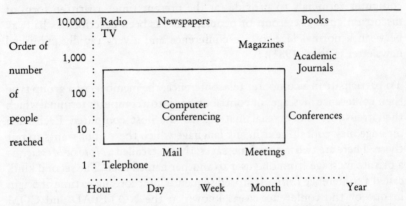

Figure 1. The Area which Computer Conferencing Covers has hitherto been Empty

The beginnings of computer conferencing are to be found in military command and control networks, the Washington-Moscow 'hot line' via telex, and the ARPAnet message system supported from defence research funds. The early research in computer conferencing began at the Augmentation Research Laboratory of Stanford Research Institute, at the Institute for the Future in California, and in the Electronic Information Exchange System (EIES) at the New Jersey Institute of Technology. From this early work, computer conferencing is now already established as a medium to aid scientific and technical work (cf. Hiltz & Turoff, 1978; Johansen, Vallee & Spangler, 1979). Several people have suggested the use of this medium to assist or even replace the traditional form of scientific publishing, that is to produce 'electronic journals'.

A few years ago, as a response to the rapidly rising costs of scholarly publishing combined with a contracting market, the idea of 'the editorial processing centre' was proposed (Bamford, 1976; Woodward et al, 1976). This centre was thought of as being a co-operative editorial office for a number of learned societies, with communication between authors, academic editors and referees facilitated by technology in the form of

2

electronic mail on-line or of machine-readable magnetic tape and discs off-line. One of the purposes underlying these investigations was to reduce the number of times that a paper has to be retyped, since retyping results in time delays, errors and high costs.

From here it is a small step to consider the final product from such an 'editorial processing centre' as being stored and disseminated, in some machine-readable form via the telecommunications network, to the ultimate user, so that every stage from initial typing to ultimate reading need not use paper at all. This is what we mean by an 'electronic journal'.

1.2 The EIES Electronic Journal Project

The first electronic journal project was established, with funding from the National Science Foundation (NSF), on the EIES network for $3\frac{1}{2}$ years from October 1976 to March 1980. Within that programme there was a project to explore a traditional form of refereed papers journal for $1\frac{1}{2}$ years, October 1978–March 1980. The planned British participation was prevented by a Post Office embargo at that time on extensive transatlantic computer-based message transition. This project did not achieve all its objectives (see the final report — Sheridan et al, 1981), but some useful learning can be gained from the problems and possible reasons as suggested by various persons involved with it (see Figure 2, which contains the present authors' conclusions based upon the available evidence).

1. Too many projects and users on EIES, resulting in variable and often long system response delays.
2. Command structure and editing system too complex for 'computer naive' users.
3. Lack of flexibility in journal procedures (e.g. only on-line input permitted, and absolute assignment of copyright required).
4. Lack of status or prestige for a hitherto unpublished 'journal' probably gave it low priority for potential authors.
5. Quality and flexibility of terminals too limited in relation to possible benefits for users (it is easy to forget how much terminals have improved since 1977-78).
6. Little use of techniques to increase involvement of user community (e.g. face-to-face meetings).
7. Project duration ($1\frac{1}{2}$ years) probably too short.

Figure 2. Problems with the 1978-80 USA Refereed Papers Journal

On the other hand, it would be wrong to suggest that the EIES project as a whole was not successful. Other types of electronic journal on the system were more fully supported:— a weekly newsletter was published and found very acceptable; an unrefereed papers journal (*Paper Fair*) received over 40 papers during six months; a structured enquiry response system among 25 scientific advisers to state legislatures was considered to be very useful.

The potential importance of electronic journals has already been pointed out by Senders, 1977, in view of the rising costs of materials, production, publishing and library facilities. Taking a much wider view of the whole process of the dissemination of scientific information (through primary and secondary publications) and of its storage and retrieval (through libraries and information services), Lancaster, 1978, has envisaged the possibilities for paperless information systems up to the year 2000. His enthusiasm may lead to some oversight of many detailed problems, but he may well not be too far in error with his general thesis and scenario. Meadows, 1980, has also considered these future possibilities in a shorter but perhaps more pragmatic and rounded review of the practical realities. A study of the scientific information system in Britain has recently been published (Royal Society, 1981), in which it is shown that this system, so long taken for granted by scientists, can no longer be regarded as stable. Recommendations are submitted for urgent consideration by the public authorities responsible. In the chapter of the report which reviews the impact of various new technologies, the electronic journal is seen as 'perhaps the most radical innovation in prospect for the primary literature'.

It is clearly desirable to gain practical experience in the UK of how such electronic journals can be operated. It is essential to evaluate their potential in both quantitative and qualitative terms, and eventually perhaps in various combinations of journal type and orientation, of scientific/technological discipline, of authorship/readership community, and of national/cultural environment.

1.3 British Library Electronic Journals Project

Shortly after the EIES Refereed Papers Journal project had started, i.e. early in 1979, the British Library Research & Development Department (BLR&DD) decided that it would be desirable to explore these concepts by establishing a project in Britain. Professor N. Moray, who had previously applied to join the NSF-funded experiment, recommended Professor B. Shackel as a possible Director and consequently an application was invited, was submitted in September 1979, was refereed in the normal way, and after due negotiation the programme was established from July 1980. The development towards the British project started with its

4

principal emphasis upon a refereed papers journal. While that remains the starting point, the proposal for the project recommended exploring various other possible uses of electronic communication networks, and this widening of the scope was supported by referees. The enlargement of the concept and scope was therefore approved, and subsequently the results of the EIES project have confirmed the validity of the broader approach proposed and adopted.

The decision to rent the software to support the research meant obtaining access to a suitable computer and, after several negotiations throughout the country, the new DEC20 at the University of Birmingham seemed most appropriate. As a result, the University of Birmingham is providing and developing the hardware and software facilities, and Loughborough University of Technology is developing the documentation, training and the information communities; thus we have organised the Birmingham and Loughborough Electronic Network Development (BLEND).

Aims

The aims of the BLEND system programme are to explore and evaluate the use of an electronic communication network as an aid to writing, submitting and refereeing papers, and also as a medium for other types of scientific and technical communication.

The approach proposed and adopted aims to be experimental rather than merely exploratory. Although we have started by getting an acceptable system into operation, the important part is thereafter to experiment with alternative methods and evaluate them properly (i.e. by valid and reliable test procedures with adequate numbers of users). Therefore, from the beginning it was planned to provide alternative means of entering papers, alternative procedures for refereeing papers, etc.

Basic Structure

The BLEND system and research programme now comprise:—

— A computer conferencing software suite ('NOTEPAD' from Infomedia Corporation) hosted in the DEC 20 computer at the University of Birmingham.

— A four-year project timescale with 3½ years on-line operation from 1 January 1981.

— Approximately 40 funded members (funds covering telephone connection time) in the first experimental community (LINC).

— Provision to bring in about four to five other unfunded communities after the first year.

— Provision for studying various types of journals and communication.

— Subject of the first journals and community to be 'Computer Human Factors'.

Procedures

The following plans and procedures for organising the programme were proposed, agreed and implemented from the beginning:—

— A series of 'information letters' to invite community members and then inform them of progress, starting from nine months before the on-line operation began.

— Face-to-face meeting of community members before start of trials use of system (with the aim of providing some training and achieving personal involvement).

— Face-to-face meetings of the community at the end of years 1, 2 and 3 to review progress and agree changes in experimental plans.

— Funded participants for the first community on Computer Human Factors (LINC) to be invited: approximately two-thirds from human sciences/ergonomics and one-third from computing/information sciences.

— Members provide terminals, project provides modem and telephone charges if needed.

— Members undertake to submit one longer paper and one shorter note ('dispatch') in each year of the programme.

— At first the procedures for submitting and refereeing papers will be very similar to traditional practice, while members become accustomed to the technology and its procedures.

— After members are familiar with the technology, formal experiments will be instituted with alternative refereeing and other procedures to explore and exploit the capabilities of the electronic medium.

— From the beginning three methods for entering papers have been provided:

  1. author or secretary directly on-line;

  2. typical typescript (with corrections) sent to Loughborough for entry via secretary and word processor;

  3. perfect typed manuscript sent to Birmingham for entry via OCR machine.

— Copyright is not assigned to the journal but authors undertake not to offer papers to conventional journals until three months after they have been archived in an electronic journal.

— When refereed papers are published in conventional journals, an agreed footnote will be included on the first page such as 'This paper has been refereed, accepted and archived (in electronic form only) in the BLR&DD experimental electronic journal *Computer Human Factors.*'

— Comprehensive assessments are to be made of costs, performance, objective patterns of behaviour and subjective experiences of users.

It was evident very early that these plans and procedures gained wide acceptance. In particular, the editors or publishers of five traditional journals asked that authors of refereed papers archived in the BLEND system should be notified of these editors' and publishers' willingness to receive such papers and to give them special attention and probably more rapid refereeing.

1.4 The Place of BLEND in the Publishing Cycle

In the spheres of publishing, libraries and information science there is a growing attention towards a whole range of electronic possibilities. Since this project has sometimes been given the epithet 'electronic publishing', which it is not, its place in relation to the complete cycle of activities involved in producing and using serials may usefully be clarified.

The Activity Cycle for a Serial

The sequence of activities, in a series of broad functional categories, is given in Figure 3. The papers submitted by authors in the LINC programme, and eventually mounted in the Poster Papers Journal or Refereed Papers Journal, are not published; they are archived in electronic form only. It is emphasised to all LINC members that, when they read a paper in the journal or take a printout of it, this paper has the status of a pre-publication draft sent to them in confidence by the author. Therefore, the BLEND-LINC programme addresses the first three activities only, above the dividing line, in Figure 3.

Authoring
Refereeing
Editor accepting
BLEND-LINC stops here

Publishing
Marketing
Distributing/delivering

Storing   — reading
Abstracting   — reading
Retrieving   — reading

Figure 3. The BLEND-LINC Place in the Activity Cycle of a Serial

---

The Author-Editing Cycle

The activities to be explored within the BLEND-LINC programme, as regards a formal refereed papers journal, are expanded in Figure 4. In the first phase of the programme it was necessary to modify and develop the system until it could tolerably subserve all these activities, so that they could be undertaken experimentally. Then the possibilities and limitations of the technology, and the improvements needed, could be investigated.

1.5 Types of Journal to be Explored

We envisaged that the types of journal and communication listed in Figure 5 should be explored during the programme.

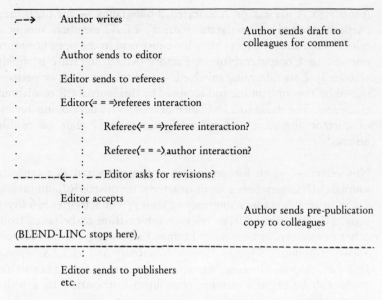

```
--→    Author writes
              :                          Author sends draft to
   .          :                          colleagues for comment
   .     Author sends to editor
   .          :
   .     Editor sends to referees
              :
         Editor<= = =>referees interaction
   .          :
   .          :    Referee<= = =>referee interaction?
   .          :
   .          :    Referee<= = =>author interaction?
   .          :
_ _ _ _ _ _ _<_ _ : _ _ Editor asks for revisions?
              :
         Editor accepts
              :                          Author sends pre-publication
              :                          copy to colleagues
(BLEND-LINC stops here)
- - - - - - - - - - - - - - - - - - - - - - - - - - - - - - - - - -
              :
         Editor sends to publishers
         etc.
```

Figure 4. The Traditional Author-Editor Cycle for Refereed Papers

The various types of journal listed in Figure 5 are outlined with some more detail below.

1. Refereed papers — writing, revising, submission, refereeing, editing and acceptance of scientific papers — the principal work envisaged for the start of the project.

2. Letters to the editor or Comments and discussions — refereed short discussion papers stimulated by an 'accepted paper', which if accepted are archived with and straight after that paper — considered as part of the principal work also.

> 1. Refereed papers — full refereeing (with anonymity) etc.
> 2. Comments and discussions — e.g. for linking with papers.
> 3. Annotated abstracts — bibliographic literature review.
> 4. LINC News — network and related information.
> 5. Bulletin — general news about current work.
> 6. Co-operative writing of papers.
> 7. Poster papers — i.e. 'paper fair' or 'free for all'.
> 8. Enquiry-answer system between experts.
> 9. Publication of complete issues or journal parts to 'readers only'.

Figure 5. The Types of Journal Envisaged at the Start

3. Annotated Abstracts or Annotated Bibliography — for organising purposes treated as a separate 'journal'. LINC members submit a critical summary of papers they have just read in the open literature relevant to Computer Human Factors (which literature is widely scattered). Less refereeing involved:— perhaps one only, or perhaps signed by the contributor and accepted by this journal editor without refereeing. The value to LINC members of such a developing 'review of current literature' information source could thus be readily assessed.

4. Newsletter — again for organising purposes treated as a separate journal. LINC members submit quarterly, for quarterly 'publication' via an open access file, a summary of their recent activities in a lively style. No refereeing. Other relevant information to be taken from other newsletters in Computer Human Factors (e.g. *Human Factors Society Computer Systems Group Newsletter* and *A.S.I.S. Special Interest Group on On-Line Interaction Newsletter*). Such a newsletter could also be printed out for photolitho distribution to a wider community.

5. BLEND Bulletin — as a development from the four information letters already sent out to the LINC members, a regular bulletin will be issued to provide network information.

6. Co-operative Writing of Papers — e.g. Developing a Manual:— in applied ergonomics for terminal design there is current active work developing manuals and checklists to aid designers and especially those selecting terminals for purchase. Pooling case-study experience from LINC members who use the manual and checklists could lead to faster development and a better end-result.

7. Poster Papers — in this type of journal any author can enter any papers so as to receive comments and revise the papers for later offering formally to the refereed papers electronic journal or to a conventional journal.

8. Enquiry-answer system between experts — another type of use would allow any accepted participant to pose specific problems so as to invite expert advice.

9. 'Readers Only' — add another category of participants i.e. 'Non-Contributing Recipients'. It is thought that many scientists and technologists working, e.g. in university computer studies departments,

in commercial manufacturers and in software houses, will become interested in this project and may wish to gain access. It would be desirable to establish this formally on an agreed basis as recipients only; for example, they would pay all terminal, connection and time costs, a fee might well be levied by BLR&DD, and they would be required to answer two or three questionnaires to provide yet further evaluation data.

It should be emphasised that there was no intention to implement all these and other ideas immediately. Clearly we needed to start with nos. 1, 4 and probably 2. All these types of journal were listed in the belief that a lively LINC would develop which would wish to explore many of these variations (and others) of its own volition; therefore, appropriate provision was made for these and other possibilities in devising the BLEND system. To share the work and experience, separate editors were made responsible for nos. 4 and 7 and others as appropriate. The detailed plans and timescale for introducing these variations and any others proposed by the LINC community were to be worked out co-operatively as the experimental programme developed.

1.6 A Summary of the History

To give an overview of the progress of the experimental programme outlined above, the main activities are presented in note form.

Sept. 1979	Invited first proposal submitted to BLR&DD.
Oct.–Jan.	First explorations and visit to USA by BLR&DD adviser.
Feb. 1980	Provisional decisions and further explorations.
Mar.	Provisional invitations to prospective LINC members. Information letters (six in all) sent at regular intervals thereafter.
Apr.	Visit to USA by Project Director to gather data.
May	Agreement upon acceptable software system.
Jun.	Research grant contracts issued.
Jul.	New timescale agreed. Staff advertisements appear.
Aug.	Visit to USA by University of Birmingham staff member to study and collect NOTEPAD Version 1.1 at Infomedia Corp.
Sept.	NOTEPAD Version 1.1 mounted on DEC 20 at Birmingham.

	Exploratory use by project team. Research Fellow appointed at LUT (from 1 Oct.).
Oct.	Documentation (Version 1) prepared. Subjective assessment questionnaires developed and issued. First projects and activities (i.e. use structure, introductory messages, first trial copy of *LINC News*) mounted ready for trial operation. Seminar meeting of 1st Information Community (LINC) held as planned on 31 October (attendance 41 out of possible 55).
15 Nov.	Trial operation of NOTEPAD Version 1.1 started.
Nov.	Subjective assessment interviews and training visits to LINC members. Trials to assess changes needed in NOTEPAD. List of essential and preferred changes to NOTEPAD agreed by project team. Agreement with Infomedia Corp. on changes possible. Research Associate appointed at Birmingham (from 1 Dec.).
Dec.	Trial operation of NOTEPAD Version 1.1 continued and interviews and 'training' visits continued.
Jan. 1981	NOTEPAD Version 1.2 received and mounted. Detailed use structure, messages, etc., and 64 members' names and passwords, etc., mounted on NOTEPAD Version 1.2. Documentation (Version 2) prepared comprising BLEND Users Guide (pp 42) & LINC Members Manual (pp 32).
15 Jan.	Full system open for use by LINC.
Jan. to Mar.	Further trials of terminals, especially microcomputers for use as intelligent terminals. Further studies of features of NOTEPAD, especially analysis programs and problems of user interaction consistency, to decide improvements to be recommended.
Apr.	Substantial changes to NOTEPAD and delivery of Version 1.3 for May and Version 2 for Aug./Sept. agreed with Infomedia (later delayed by problems at Infomedia).
Jun.	First evaluation survey of progress using structured interviews by telephone.
Jun.–Jul.	Structured interview survey by telephone.
Aug.	First papers submitted and Poster Papers Journal begins.
14 Dec.	Second LINC face-to-face meeting.

15–18 Dec.	BLR&DD programme of public seminars by BLEND team.
15 Feb. 1982	Software version 2.1 (specially enhanced) open to all. Documentation completely revised and issued to all (Version 3).
Jun.	Second community starts — W. Midlands region of Microelectronics Education Programme.
1 Oct.	First number of Refereed Papers Journal *Computer Human Factors*.
Oct.	LINC Members' teleconferences to discuss future plans.
23 Nov.	Third LINC face-to-face meeting.
Jan. 1983	Purchase of advanced microcomputers for small sub-group of volunteers approved by BLR&DD.
Feb.	Third community starts — UK Library Schools, as 'readers only' for teaching purposes.
Mar.	Extension of programme to four years approved by BLR&DD.
Apr.	Demonstrations on-line to BLEND at Stanford University (USA) and at INRIA (France).
1 May	Second number of Refereed Papers Journal *Computer Human Factors*.
1 May	*References, Abstracts & Annotations Journal* started.
24–26 May	BLR&DD programme of public seminars by BLEND team.
1 Jun.	Approval for two new communities to join BLEND — a Biotechnology Consortium and FERN (Further Education Research Network).
7–9 Jun.	Demonstrations on-line to BLEND at IATUL Conference, Essen (Germany).
Sept.	Demonstrations on-line to BLEND at IFIP Congress, Paris.
1 Aug.	*Software Reviews* journal on-line in BLEND started by LINC Member Dr. Thomas Green.
Dec.	Alvey Directorate accept invitation to try BLEND system.
20 Dec.	Fourth LINC face-to-face meeting.

2   SOFTWARE ENHANCEMENTS TO THE BLEND SYSTEM

2.1 Basing an Electronic Journal on Computer Teleconferencing

The interest in the development of electronic journals, and the need for research from the users' viewpoint, led to the decision that an early start should be made on studying actual use by users. Thus, to save three to five years of development and cost and to gain information other than intuitive reflection to act as a firm basis for future development, it was decided to start with the best possible software suite and enhance it.

The idea of making editorial processing more efficient by connecting authors, referees and editors together via an electronic communication medium (Bamford, 1976; Woodward, 1976; Woodward et al, 1976) provides a historical lead to starting with computer teleconferencing. Another reason for computer teleconferencing being a suitable basis for initial research and development comes from the communication needs of a scientific community. These needs span from the most formal communication, the refereed papers journal disseminating and archiving research, through to the informal communication such as requests for papers and notes about visits to conferences (see Figure 6). Viewing an electronic journal as part of the whole communication fabric of a scientific community suggests the need for a software suite to facilitate many kinds and levels of communication.

Refereed papers journals	Formal
Bulletins	:
Conference proceedings	:
Conference papers (spoken)	:
Pre-publication draft circulation	:
Seminars	:
Work messages	:
Chit-chat	Informal

Figure 6. Some of the Different Communications in a Scientific Community

There is one further argument for basing an experimental electronic journal on a software suite flexible enough to allow more than one communication level, style and procedure. This is that no-one could (in 1980) predict what users might want from an electronic journal. There are many hypotheses about this. To give one oft quoted example, speeding up journal production is cited as an advantage (CEC 1979); but if journals are archiving devices for status, then speed may not be a critical factor — quality and the test of time for theories may be more important. Thus an electronic journal may be an entirely different type of entity.

2.2 NOTEPAD Teleconferencing Suite

Surveys by the Chairman of the BLR&DD's New Technology Group (Professor P. Kirstein), and by Professor B. Shackel separately, suggested using a teleconferencing suite rather than a message system and bulletin board, and the NOTEPAD software suite rather than the EIES system used in the USA electronic journal experiment. The NOTEPAD software system was in commercial use and offered with full support, having been developed through two successive previous systems FORUM and PLANET. EIES on the other hand was available only by special arrangement and without full maintenance support. One key factor identified in both surveys was the evaluation that NOTEPAD was easier for naive users than EIES, and this was subsequently confirmed by the report on the EIES electronic journal (Sheridan et al, 1981).

2.3 Development Procedure

Although it was generally agreed that NOTEPAD was the most 'user-friendly' software suite available at that time for computer teleconferencing, it was to be put to use for rather different purposes.

The initial organisation of the NOTEPAD system for BLEND use was a direct consequence of analysis and discussions by interested parties. Thus it rested on the 'expert' opinion of those experienced in computer teleconferencing and in editorial procedure. The first enhancements were also developed by way of the 'expert' opinion of members of the BLEND team in conjunction with initial periods of trials use.

Before the main use of NOTEPAD in the experimental programme of electronic journals, a period of three months was allowed for trials by all users who had the necessary equipment. The users were computer specialists or human factors specialists (psychologists and ergonomists) who were active in the field of Computer Human Factors. Their initial reaction to the system as naive users was qualified by expertise in this field. Thus the expert opinion of the project team and the 'expert' users' reactions contributed to the first set of enhancements; these were partially implemented in the version of the software made available for the start of the main three-year experimental programme.

During the course of main use, developments and revisions continued. Necessarily, in a system with expanding facilities whose use was hypothesised rather than actual, expert opinion continued to play a part. However, evidence for different enhancements came from many other more formal sources, as presented in the following list:

— observations by a researcher of first-time use to see what expectations the users had and what problems were encountered

— analysis of HELP requests by phone, answerphone and as messages in the BLEND system

— structured interviewing via the telephone to obtain a 'snapshot' of attitudes and thoughts regarding use and non-use of the system (Pullinger, 1982, 1984c)

— formal controlled experiments on certain aspects including part of the dialogue, structuring of papers and aids to reading on-line

— analysis of use data collected by the software.

More generalised formal experiments were also planned to assess fully the facilities needed by a software suite to support electronic journals. This process for the evolutionary design and enhancement of a system is similar to that recommended in Eason, 1982.

2.4 Enhancements

The initial development and subsequent research quickly illustrated four major areas in which difficulty was experienced.

1. The wish to accomplish different tasks while logged into the computer.

2. 'Knowing where one is' in the database structure.

3. Consistency in concept and command structure.

4. Handling large pieces of text.

Each will be discussed with examples where applicable.

1. *The wish to accomplish different tasks while logged into the computer*

The structure of NOTEPAD is so designed that each commercial organisation or group would have a separate secure area, with a password, (called a Project).

The BLEND Project Director initiated, after discussion, a structure which placed different types of work activity in different areas, for example writing papers in one, reading journals in another, exchanging news in yet another. Almost immediately it was discovered that while some users did separate these different functions operationally, others would log in and wish to be provided with a facility to enable easy and rapid passing between the areas.

Consequently an additional level was introduced to meet the needs of some users (see Figure 7). To establish whether the expressed need for this was in fact justified, a data analysis package was introduced.

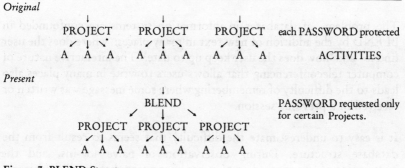

Figure 7. BLEND Structure

Questions may be asked such as 'In general, do users log in to accomplish one thing, for example referee a paper or read a journal?' or 'Do users go to a terminal and then accomplish everything relating to the BLEND system in one session?' Answers depend on many factors including working style, work situation and access to terminal equipment, but preliminary inspection shows that while some users only log into one Project in one on-line session, others log into many. Thus this facility to move between Projects is both needed and useful, provided that it does not interfere with use by those not requiring it.

Introducing another level, however, brings other problems such as 'knowing where one is' and 'knowing what there is to see' which are discussed next.

2. 'Knowing where one is' in the database structure

Knowing where one is and where to go in a two-level hierarchical tree structure may seem a trivial problem. However, one experiment in viewdata illustrated the difficulties of searching with goal acquisition in just two levels which caused much distress to the subjects (Van Nes and Van der Heijden, 1980). It does seem, though, that a two-level system appears optimum for moderate-sized hierarchical systems, both from a small user survey (Cole, 1981) which showed that this is the preferred number for many office filing systems and from an experiment on menu-based on-line search (Miller, 1981). The hierarchical system of Projects and Activities in BLEND is comparable in size to those investigated in the studies. These show that breadth is preferred over depth for an increase in the number of sections, i.e. that more Projects and Activities are to be preferred to introducing a third level.

The problems of databases in information systems are confounded in BLEND by the addition of new text in many places: 'where does the user find it?' and 'how does the user keep up to date?' The interactive nature of computer teleconferencing that allows users to write in many places also leads to the difficulty of remembering where some message was written or received in a previous session.

It is easy to underestimate the difficulty that seems to result from the database structure. During observation of naive log-ins, and the questioning of experienced users, it has been noted that the difficulties do not necessarily diminish with familiarity. Even when one 'knows where one is', there may still be difficulty incurred in getting to where one then wishes to go. Handling both the conceptual structure of the database and the commands necessary have proved awkward for some users, and several alternative user aids and support have been necessary (as are frequently recommended but rarely supplied cf. Damodaran, 1976).

Further possible 'knowing' difficulties lie in the nature of the tasks performed on the system: sending and receiving messages, writing papers, editing, refereeing and reading. By long-term adaptation to both the tools and process of using paper, we are used to a glance at pigeon-holes to see what mail there is, with the envelope size, shape and colour frequently

18

enabling assessment of the priority of dealing with the contents even before opening. A skim through a journal will give us the idea of how much effort (time, difficulty, etc.) will be required for a particular paper. These and other tasks are easy to stop temporarily in the middle and, with another glance, see how far we are through and estimate the time to the end of the task and then pick up and continue.

The computer medium does not allow many of these procedures developed between man and his tools over many years, and it poses problems that are now beginning to be considered. The VDU screen is, as it were, a very small window into a very large library.

Electronic mail has treated some of these problems in having a mailbox presented to the user with informative envelopes when he logs in (see, for example, discussion in Uhlig, 1981). The user may then place the messages in his own categorisation and database (including a waste-bin if desired!).

Several substantial attempts have been made to improve the locational sense of databases that many people build into their office systems with the aim of knowing what there is, and where and how to travel to it (Bolt, 1979; Spence and Apperley, 1982).

Computer teleconferencing with its concept of an ongoing discussion with conference entries gradually accumulating over many hours or several years has a rather different structure from electronic mail and presents difficulties for users with many conferences. Some computer conferencing suites (e.g. COM, Palme & Enderin, 1982) have a flexible order of conferences with those containing new messages being placed at the top. Some users, however, complain about the directiveness of such a system and of never quite knowing where they are.

To summarise, possible difficulties for the user are:

1. knowing where one is;

2. knowing where and how one can go;

3. knowing what there is new to see;

4. knowing what what-there-is-to-see involves;

5. knowing whether one has seen everything;

6. knowing where one saw something previously.

In the BLEND system there have been a few enhancements to obviate some of these difficulties, though this is only a beginning in tackling the problems experienced. Far more radical innovations are needed for the future. In 'knowing where one is', four principles have been used:

1. reinforcing redundancy;

2. help when requested;

3. returning to a known point and starting again;

4. operating from one conceptual position.

To give an example of the principle of reinforcing redundancy consider the many different cues that are used for any set of objects. For example, journals in a pile may be remembered in several ways, colour ('the red one'), distinguishing marks ('the one with a coffee stain'), and size ('the big one'). These are reinforced by each search in the process of doing other tasks. With computer text messages this principle is applied by giving short redundant information to remind the user, possibly subconsciously, where he/she is. The Project Title is added above each Activity Title to form a pair whenever each is displayed, and a page-header facility has been introduced to set a running header (for printer or VDU). A further proposal (not able to be implemented) was for the Activity just left to be displayed in order to orientate movements around each Project.

Most important for the user is probably the facility to ask 'Where am I?'. Pressing three keys (two of them the Return or Enter key) sends a statement 'You are in Project ... Activity ... '.

Casual observation of computers in use shows that many people, occasional and long-standing users, have a 'let's start again' fallback position which they find helpful. It is hence useful to have a facility to jump out of what one is doing to a *known point* and permit this restart. Accordingly commands have been implemented and made consistent so as to return the user to such start points. Subsequently, annotated printouts of some individuals' use clearly indicate that they wished to adopt such a strategy, which they were then able to do.

3. Consistency in concept and command structure

Watching a young person using the telephone for the first few times can be highly instructive. Most of us are so familiar with the process that we forget that it is a *learnt* one, that the protocol is different, that we speak differently as is necessary without non-verbal cues and that the medium affects the content of the message. For example, one has to give a verbal cue to indicate that one has finished speaking and that the other person has an opportunity. In normal conversation this is non-verbal.

The difference in the conceptual framework of the child as a naive user of the telephone and the experienced user is analogous to the difference found between naive users of computer systems and the experts. There is, however, an important distinction. In the child's case, there is clearly no alternative solution to the mismatch of conceptual frameworks than that of learning and adopting the widespread convention, whereas in the computer system there are often alternatives available.

One such example occurred in the BLEND system, which is hosted on a DEC20. Commands to the computer are usually ended by pressing the Return or Enter key. Before the command is completed, help and editing facilities may be invoked by control and other special characters. One of the help facilities is obtained by pressing just the question mark '?', which is regarded as such a character, i.e. not as a command itself. The operational strategy for naive users in NOTEPAD might be stated — 'End all commands by pressing the Return key except for control characters'. Many naive users include the control and special characters in the categorisation of 'command' and hence create the above strategy. Including them in the category of command, however, led to a direct conflict in the system so that users responding in one particular place with a question mark and Return (?CR) were logged out of the system. The command, as their operational strategy viewed it, was consistent with all they.knew and yet was in conflict with how the system operated. The conflict was resolved by allowing *both* to be acceptable, despite the difficulty expressed by the system designers, particularly with the solving of the 'read-ahead' store of characters. The user could type a question mark followed immediately by a Return, or not, as chosen; after a delay, however, if a Return was typed then it was taken in Read Ahead mode of the host computer to be the next command. In this way the operational strategy of both expert and naive users could be maintained.

It is thus important for systems designers to know what type of conceptual framework the users are likely to bring to their interactions. Gringas, 1976, has shown that computer systems analysts have psychological self-images that are very similar to their image of an ideal user of the system, which can lead to a poor fit with actual users.

There have been several attempts at classifications of users which have enabled concentration on the particular needs of each group (for example see Eason, Damodaran, Stewart, 1974; Gaines, 1981; Maguire, 1982). The closest classification to describe the present users of BLEND might be 'casual', i.e. those who only use the system occasionally. Cuff, 1980, has discussed the dialogue requirements and other needs for such users. However he particularly emphasises casual users who are naive, and the problems of those who are otherwise (e.g. those who are computer 'experts' for other systems) not addressed.

The first community to use BLEND was a collection of human factors and computer academics (the Loughborough Information Network Community — LINC) and so in experience they range from the most naive to the most experienced in the use of computer systems. However, only logging into the system between twice a week or once a fortnight brings some problems irrespective of computer experience.

The naive users bring no understanding with them to the system and make the best rational rule available to explain the system's behaviour, which will often be confounded (as in the example above about what it is that constitutes a command). Experienced users frequently have substantial preconceived ideas and have already learned many command structures. To learn a new structure not often used (relative to other systems) would in any case impose a high memory load, but they have to cope with the frustration that they know exactly what they want to do with the system conceptually but do not know which commands to give to accomplish it (see Figure 8).

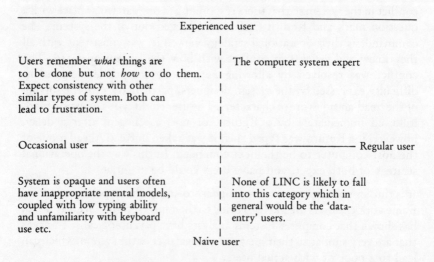

Figure 8. LINC Members on the Left of the Diagram can have Problems Whether Naive or Experienced in Computer Systems

Thus for this kind of 'occasional' user it is suggested that features such as high consistency in the command structure with ease of use should take priority over a wide range of available commands at each point. The need for conceptual consistency throughout all related areas of the system should take priority even sometimes at the cost of an individual facility.

4. Handling large pieces of text

In the past, large pieces of text in a computer have usually been treated in a single lump. When the text was presented for reading or editing, the computer scrolled through until the appropriate point. Whereas there are many situations where this is appropriate, it is not so when editing on-line at 300 baud (a full-length paper of 6,000 words takes about 20 minutes to be transmitted down the line), nor is it appropriate for reading. Researchers seeking information from text have many different purposes (cf. Harri-Augstein, Smith & Thomas, 1982) and thus adopt differing strategies. To give one example, when viewing academic journal papers many readers adopt a pattern: Author — Title — Abstract — Conclusions — References — Methodology. Viewing papers on-line through a VDU also requires a way of handling the text to facilitate the jumping around required by many readers.

Academic papers are sent to the host computer at Birmingham by a variety of procedures. These include sending a typed copy for an Optical Character Reader, an edited typed copy for entry by a word-processing operator, direct on-line typing and sending a file prepared on a micro-computer or other terminal.

Beforehand, NOTEPAD was designed to receive messages, which as conference entries could not be altered or replaced, and then to display them in sequence. The requirement to be able to handle text in the form described above for writing and editing, and to allow flexibility to a reader for displaying, had the following consequences:

— For consistency the command to end one entry and start another in the middle of a paper should be the same as ending a single entry, and the same whether writing on the system, in a text editor or some other procedure.

— A single paragraph should be able to be accessed for editing and then replaced.

— A single paragraph or section of text should be easily accessible for reading.

— Copying text-files in the software and moving them around should preserve the paragraph structure.

A suitable structure was accomplished (after considerable negotiation with the system providers and designers) and additional programs written to aid editing and reading. A choice of text editors is available and readers may display the text on a VDU by stepping back and forward in paragraph-sized chunks, by giving the 'page' number, or giving a heading, e.g. 'Conclusions'. Already the use data illustrate that some members exhibit a 'jumping around' strategy whereas others read linearly through a paper. The text may also be displayed on a printer, setting a short header and having pages automatically numbered.

The relationship between this kind of software, to support reading for skimming and scanning, and the structure of the paper itself is the subject of ongoing research, since there is *a priori* no reason for only permitting linear structure for text of journal paper length.

The problems identified above in knowing where one is and knowing what the task involves apply also to the situation in individual papers being read on a VDU screen. It is expected that technology will evolve so that cues will be available which will be equivalent to seeing the scope of the contents. However, at the present time the problem is similar to viewing a paper through a $4'' \times 2''$ window. Suggested solutions for this have varied from a visual emulation of a pair of pages open with indication of relation to the other pages (Benest & Jones, 1982) to a full tree structure access.

2.5 BLEND Software for Reading Papers

The first new facility introduced in the BLEND system to aid reading of papers was built into the NOTEPAD software by Infomedia Corporation at the request of the BLEND project team. On setting up the list of entries to be read, the user can also specify if he/she wishes to use the 'step' function. This allows him/her to step backwards and forwards through the paper. After each entry is displayed, the user has the option of going on to the next entry, back to the previous one, repeating the one already displayed (used, for instance, if on reading the entry he/she realises a printed copy would be useful) or aborting the reading session. The main differences between this and the more usual methods are:

1. The facility to move backwards.

2. The facility to stop the reading process in the middle of a list of entries or a paper.

3. The text is displayed entry by entry instead of stopping when the screen gets full.

4. For recognised terminals, the screen is cleared and the text displayed from the top. This means that the user reads still text, not continuously moving text.

Although the step function provides these additional facilities a utility program was written to enable the users to adopt further their chosen reading strategy for hard-copy papers. In addition to replicating the facilities provided in the NOTEPAD step function, an additional command to go to any entry by giving the entry number was implemented. Thus the user can have random access to the whole paper. The command to go back to the previous entry has the meaning 'go back to the entry most recently displayed'; further use of this subcommand displays the entry displayed before that one until the original first entry is arrived at. Also a string search command was introduced to scan the first lines of the entries. Thus it is possible to go straight to 'conclusions' for example. Three additional facilities were therefore added:

5. The facility to jump around the text.

6. A command to return to the previously displayed section of text.

7. A string search on first lines of entries to enable jumping to named section headings.

This utility allows readers to use reading strategies approaching their normal ones. For those that go through the paper in a specified order, the entries may be called up by use of the string search command. It is for this purpose that the command was devised. The search examines the text on the first two lines of each entry thus avoiding finding references to the title in other parts of the text. If the section titles are not standard, for example when there is no 'conclusions' or 'discussion' section, the reader always has the option of displaying the contents list in entry 2 first and then going to the appropriate section.

The facility to go back to the entry previously displayed may be used when looking at another part of the text and then returning. For example, checking a reference, diagram or figure and then returning to the text from where it was referenced. This might be considered the electronic equivalent of keeping your finger in the page.

A summary of the commands provided is shown in Figure 9.

Abort	— End running of program
Forward, Return	— Display next entry
Back, Previous	— Display entry most recently seen
Repeat	— Display current entry again
Number of entry	— Display the entry of that number
"Quoted string"	— Display next entry with the title containing the given string
"	— Repeat last string request

Figure 9. Summary of Commands Available in the READ Program

2.6 BLEND Software for Refereeing Papers

When a paper is refereed, comments are written about the paper in a report to the journal editor. The act of refereeing is not just reading the paper and writing a report; some referees like to write on the script itself, making notes and marks in the margins. If these notes are to be passed on to the editor, it is important that they are referenced to the relevant line or paragraph. In an electronic journal the script may not be supplied as hard copy and so this process is non-trivial.

Software has been developed in the BLEND system to allow the referees to make comments and 'marks' attached to entries in the script, thus going towards replicating the activity described above. Every entry in the paper may have a comment tied to it which is available to be read on request. The referee may make a comment which is then tied to the entry currently being viewed. To maintain confidentiality, the comments and paper are only available to the referee.

The software permits access to the comment independently of the entries; commands are available to the referee to step through the comments one by one, to display all the comments, to see individual ones as well as commands to remove, replace and create them.

Another thing that referees sometimes wish to do is to make a mark in the margin in order that the section can easily be picked out again. This facility was also included in the software. One command marks the current entry so that each time the entry is displayed there is also a short note at the bottom 'Entry Marked'. Many entries may have marks and these can be displayed all together or one at a time quite independently of the rest.

The structure of the text and marks may be represented by something like Figure 10.

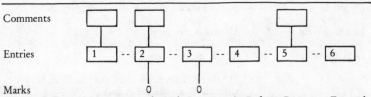

Figure 10. Entry, Comment and Mark Structure in Referee Program. Example shows Textual Comments and Marks (or Flags) Tied to Particular Entries

The referees may read the paper in their chosen manner and make comments as they go along. Particular sections to which they might wish to refer later, or might wish the editor to refer, may be marked for easy access later. The journal editor may be given a synopsis of, or access to, these in-script comments as well as any other report conveyed in private.

It should be noted that this only goes part of the way in mimicking the facilities available to the hard-copy referee. Comments and marks are only specific to the entry and cannot for instance be attached to a particular word or phrase. Thus it may be difficult to underline spelling mistakes, circle a part of a figure, etc. On the other hand there are advantages in refereeing on-line which are not available to the hard-copy referee. One of these is that communication with the editor can be faster and more of a dialogue than a report. Questions may be asked as if the script were in front of both of them. Such a dialogue, in a conferencing system, may be synchronous (i.e. both present at the same time) or asynchronous (i.e. the dialogue extending over a period of time with only one using the system at any one time). Also more unusual refereeing possibilities exist such as multi-way discussions between the editor and more than one referee, again with a soft copy of the script, comments and marks in front of them all. Possibilities also exist for putting the referees in touch with the original authors, maybe anonymously.

Figure 11 lists the additional commands available to the referee in this Activity.

Details of the development procedure of the refereeing utility software may be found in Maude and Dodd, 1983.

Comment	— Make a comment on current entry
See	— Display the comment tied to current entry
Delete Comment	— Delete the comment tied to current entry
Overwrite	— Replace the comment tied to current entry
Last Comment	— Display last comment
Next Comment	— Display next comment
	(These two commands allow the referee to browse through the comments made.)
Every Comment	— List all comments made
Mark	— Mark current entry
Delete Mark	— Remove mark on current entry
Last Mark	— Display last entry marked
Next Mark	— Display next entry marked
	(These two comments allow the referee to browse through the marked entries.)
Every Mark	— List all marked entries

Figure 11. Additional Commands in Refereeing

2.7 BLEND Software for Browsing

On 1 May 1983, the BLEND experimental programme started the on-line *References, Abstracts and Annotations Journal* (RAAJ). This contains a database of bibliographic references in the subject area of Computer Human Factors up to 1981 and more recent references and authors' abstracts from selected journals.

It was recognised that the software needed for browsing the RAAJ would need to be similar to that for refereeing in that comments (annotations) must be attached to the entry concerned. Facilities for moving about the abstracts would also be similar; however, some features needed to be changed. The most fundamental change to the software was that of searching. When reading and refereeing a paper it is important to be able to find headings and titles, and so the first two lines are searched when a string search command is performed. In an abstracts journal it is important to be able to search for keywords, authors, dates etc. The database was, therefore, set up with keywords on a special line(s) which is indicated by an asterisk. Each of these lines also includes the entry number. When a keyword search is done, all the keyword lines containing the keyword are displayed and the users may then choose the particular entry by number. This and the other reading commands may be used to browse through the database.

Comments may be seen just as in the referee utility, and also browsed by use of the next comment and last comment commands.

It was expressed as important, also, to be able to browse through comments by certain commentators whose value judgement is highly respected by the browser, thus filtering out some of the annotations. Thus string searches may also be performed on comments.

Marking references is useful too as this may be used to make a note of important references as the user browses, in order to take a copy at a later point in time. Thus when the browsing session is finished, the marked abstracts (possibly together with their associated annotations) may be printed out, reviewed or stored in the user's microcomputer.

Another major difference between this software and the refereeing utility is that the comments are not confidential but have public access. If a reader wishes to make an annotation it is sent as a private note to the sub-editor and then placed in the database in the appropriate format.

As this is in the public domain, marks have to be personalised so as to avoid confusion. The marks are associated with a particular individual and only exist for one session.

2.8 Monitoring Software Use

One of the objectives of the BLEND programme is an evaluation of the use of the software and consequently a monitor has been built into all the software mentioned to log the actions taken by individuals. The monitor records what commands are made, which entries are read and in what order and the starting and finishing time. To maintain confidentiality the referees' comments are not recorded in the log.

With the data recorded it will be possible to analyse the users' reading habits on-line as well as the use of the various commands provided.

2.9 Discussion

The changes made from the original NOTEPAD software for reading are apparently quite small. However, we believe that these changes make a much more usable system allowing the readers to read papers in a style to which they are more accustomed.

The use log will provide more information as to the reading habits of BLEND users. The analysis of these data will take place at a later date and the results will be subsequently published; however, during an initial trial experiment it was noted that some people are quite prepared to read journal articles on-line in a linear fashion.

The philosophy behind the design of these software utilities has been to provide users with software tools which enable them to take actions similar to those taken when dealing with hard-copy articles. Thus readers can skip around a paper in any order they wish, referees can make comments and marks in the 'margin' and browsers going through a set of references, abstracts and annotations can mark those required for future reference. In this way the growing communities of users of the BLEND system can more easily comprehend the facilities that are being made available to them.

One can conceive many other possibilities when faced with computer technology such as direct referencing to other papers available on the system (e.g. on seeing a reference the user could immediately get a copy of that paper); voice-over comments allowing referees to express their opinions verbally, the comments being tied to the particular place in the text; diagrams that move; automated sorting of a paper into the individual user's preferred order of reading, e.g. title, abstract, conclusions, etc. Such facilities are too varied to provide as a matter of course in an experimental system. When dealing with a voluntary and busy community it is important that there is only a small learning overhead before the system can be used, therefore the facilities implemented are not too unusual in approach. These other features need further evaluative research to establish their acceptability and potential value, so work is being done in parallel on some of them.

3   JOURNALS AND ORGANISATIONAL ASPECTS

3.1 The Design and Presentation of the *Computer Human Factors* Journal

There are many ways in which text is handled in computer systems for subsequent display to users at a VDU screen or a printer. Included among these are the usual computer file full of text whose display is controlled by manipulation of keys by the user — often only 'pause' and 'release pause' — and the much more structured information found on viewdata systems such as British Telecom's 'Prestel' service. The initial concern for BLEND was in how to present a *journal* on the screen with its multiplicity of papers and rather different sections of material, for example the editorial, a paper, a letter to the editor. As well as the matter of presentation, there is the aspect of how the reader is directed around the text. This is usually done by typographic cues to aid skimming and scanning and by referencing to page numbers and diagram or figure numbers. Many of the standard strategies developed by scholarly communication and publishing in general raise questions to be answered afresh in an electronic medium.

3.1.1 To Issue or Accumulate?

The first important difference between electronic storage and paper as media for communicating papers is in the way that the journal articles are distributed. In the former, at the present time, they are placed in a computer (by either acting as a host or transferred around a distributed network), and those with suitable terminals can enter at their convenience to see the articles. When they are in paper form they are sent out to subscribers and libraries at particular times, each issue containing a number of articles. It will be immediately apparent that the electronic medium enables us to move from the concept of distributed issues to that of making an article available to a prospective reader as soon as it is ready.

It has been speculated that there are good reasons for doing this, particularly as the issue concept has developed from resource limitations. The limitations of the resources available to the publisher lie in the cost of raw materials in publication, the cost of paper and ink, etc., the cost of setting up the production run, which is more conveniently done and cheaper in a block lot rather than individual papers, and in the cost of distribution, which is also cheaper in issues rather than as separate papers.

This limiting of expenditure has largely determined the issue concept. There are other factors about scholarly publishing too that make this convenient. The limitation due to cost on the number of pages in each issue works to the advantage of the publisher, when there is a healthy flow of prepared articles available and these can be set up without undue haste or last-minute hasty proof-reading.

Some authors view the delaying of publishing articles as desirable because it enables changes to be made in a wider perspective in hindsight and overview, after the initial excitement of the research or topic which they described has faded a little. Thus the printing queue alone can be regarded as favourable for maintaining quality, reducing ephemera and ensuring that papers have a more lasting archival status.

There are some advantages for the reader too. There are not many journals in which every article is of interest to a particular reader and it would appear that in general the situation veers towards the reader looking for just one or two articles of interest in a journal central to the field of expertise. It may be easier for the reader to find these articles of interest quickly when the papers are distributed occasionally in issue form. If, however, they are distributed to a library, the picture would remain the same for a reader who regularly browses the journal — instead of an issue there would be a stack of articles in some form (but they would probably require substantially more archiving work by the library staff).

Thus there are several reasons which might suggest that an issue form may be desirable even when it is not totally determined by the limitations of resources (see also Figure 12).

Author	Editorial centre/publisher	Reader
Delay leads to wider perspective, higher quality.	Reduction of cost of materials. Convenience of organisation. Reduction of pre-run costs. Reduction of distribution costs. Prediction of issues because articles in hand.	Convenience of search and access both personal and in a library.

Figure 12. Advantages in Issuing a Group of Articles

We should also present the reasons for having an 'accumulated' journal of articles rather than one distributed in issues, particularly taking note of the electronic medium. We have already noted that in a typical journal issue only one or two articles may be of interest to a reader. In the electronic medium there is no physical restriction on the size of an issue, which means that the accumulated articles journal may have a far greater number of articles of relevance to the reader. With the aid of suitable software programs to facilitate searching, this may well lead to enhanced access to articles of interest. Arguments put forward also emphasise the advantages of the speed of knowing what other work is being done in the field and in the subsequent possibility of sharing in a 'live' aspect of the research. The latter aspect is particularly felt by some, because the present delays before articles appear in print (of the order of one to two years) mean that the content is effectively describing past and completed research work or ideas, rather than providing opportunities for other researchers or thinkers to participate in a current debate. Thus a journal in which articles appear as they are ready after the editorial process could provide better opportunity to be aware of, and participate in, the current research or thinking.

However, in the EIES electronic journal experiment (see Sheridan et al, 1981), it was discovered that with the newsletter, readers expressed a preference for 'publication' on a set date on a regular basis. The readers could then be assured that when they logged in at a certain date there was a new 'issue' to read. It would seem to be a strategy to reduce the costs in a cost-benefit trade-off, so that readers need not regularly access the computer just to see whether there had been any new material, but could enter knowing that on certain occasions there would be some of interest. In the BLEND electronic journal experiment, this thinking was continued to the consideration of reducing the cost to the reader of entering the system and searching it for new articles. Therefore, both the newsletter (*LINC News*) and the Refereed Papers Journal (*Computer Human Factors*) were made available in issue form.

Nevertheless, the logical reasons in favour of accumulating articles are such that the guidance from one experiment should not totally determine the procedures in the BLEND system. Therefore, it was decided that the Poster Papers Journal and the Bulletin should be accumulative. The reason for adopting both alternatives was to enable a comparison of readers' attitudes to the whole question — thus maintaining the basic aim of this experimental programme, to find out what is best for the actual users of the information, who are the journal readers in this particular case.

The cumulative nature of the Poster Papers Journal means that when a large number of articles has accumulated, the journal is too cumbersome to use easily on the BLEND system. Thus, after a certain set period, or when a set number of articles are made available in the journal area, then some must be transferred to a more long-term archive leaving only the most recent articles in the journal.

3.1.2 Presentation of the Journal

One of the strategies which many readers use in their search for articles of interest in journals is to read the contents list. As an early policy decision it was agreed to start (but not necessarily keep) a mechanism which as far as possible enabled readers to use the strategies which they had developed over the years. Thus the contents list was maintained to help the reader together with producing sets of articles in issues.

When entering the BLEND-LINC system, the reader is presented with a list of options which include the mnemonics for the journals: BULLETIN, POSTER, CHF1, CHF2, CHF3, RAAJ, SR, and CC1-2. When one of these is selected by typing the mnemonic, the reader is immediately presented with the equivalent of a contents list (Figure 13).

---

1. *Editorial* 1 October 1982	[E7.L87]
2. Shackel B. *The BLEND System – Programme of Study*	[E72.L986]
3. Morrison D. & Green T. *Adaptive Methods in Recognising Speech*	[E45.L575]
4. Bason G. & Wright P. *Detour Routes to Usability*	[E45.L818]
5. Dodd P. *Computer Conferencing Aided Learning*	[E26.L369]
6. Review — Wilson P. on Galitz W.O. 'H.F. in Office Automation'	[E14.L245]
7. Discussions/Questions by Readers on 1. Editorial & general aspects	
8. Discussions/Questions by Readers on 2. Shackel paper	
9. Discussions/Questions by Readers on 3. Morrison & Green paper	
10. Discussions/Questions by Readers on 4. Bason & Wright paper	
11. Discussions/Questions by Readers on 5. Dodd dispatch	
12. Discussions/Questions by Readers on 6. Wilson book review	

Figure 13. The Contents List of *Computer Human Factors* Issue 1

Each of the journals contains this contents list and indeed the structure of BLEND, which is based on the NOTEPAD computer teleconferencing software suite, makes this list automatically prepared and presented to the reader. This is one of the features that was noted by the Project Director-Designate in his visit to the USA in April 1980 (Shackel, 1980) while reviewing the possibilities of NOTEPAD as the basic software.

To remind the reader of this section of some of the nomenclature, the software suite NOTEPAD calls each of the major areas, such as the Poster Papers Journal, CHF1 (*Computer Human Factors* Issue No. 1), a 'Project' and when the reader goes into a 'Project' a list of 'Activities' is presented, each of which contains an article, editorial or discussion. Thus some journals have been mapped (as it were) on to separate Projects as issues and others accumulated into Projects. Figure 14 summarises a few of these to point out the way in which they are handled.

Computer Human Factors	— Issued at intervals when several articles are ready. — Each issue is one Project. — Thus there are several Projects, CHF1, CHF2, etc., each with a contents list visible when journal is entered. — Editor Professor B. Shackel.
Poster Papers Journal	— Accumulative store of articles. — One Project to which is added each article, when ready. — When too many articles are in the Project, then older ones are archived in STACK-POSTER. — Editor T. Maude.
Bulletin	— Accumulative store of articles about BLEND-LINC. — One Project to which is added each article, when ready. — Too many articles not anticipated. — Editor D.J. Pullinger.
LINC News	— Accumulative store of 'issues' over one year. — One Activity containing many short items. — Each set of items added monthly. — Contents list has to be prepared as item. — Editor D.J. Pullinger.

Figure 14. The Project and Activity Mapping of Four 'Journals'

3.1.3 The Structure of an Article

After choosing one of the menu choices in the contents list of a journal, the reader enters the Activity containing the article and is able to access its sections. The word 'sections' is used advisedly in that it is well-known that readers of articles do not generally start at the beginning and go through to the end. Although there has, so far, been no definitive research on the way that readers handle journal articles, various search strategies are known to be used. Some of these involve a series of filters starting with the contents list and continuing through the abstract, introduction and results, whereas others use the abstract and reference list first. More than one strategy uses skimming and scanning through the article, flicking pages. What all have in common is the use of reader expectation as to the structure of the article and various typographic cues to aid the search, whether in finding a section or scanning the headings or diagrams. In the BLEND-LINC journal *Computer Human Factors*, these two aspects, reader expectation of the structure and typographic cues, contributed to the particular editorial policy adopted.

Each Activity contains a sequential number of message slots called 'Entries'. The software NOTEPAD included some facilities for retrieval of individual, or groups of, Entries, which enabled different sections of the text to be accessed. Hence, splitting an article into small sections to be placed in the Entry slots would enable the reader to access small parts of the text. The limitation on the number of lines of text visible on a VDU screen (Cathode Ray Tube) is generally about 24 and so the Entries were limited to this number of lines, thus preventing the text from scrolling off the top of the screen. Indeed, the recommendation to authors in the *LINC Manual* went further to suggest that each paragraph should be considered a separate Entry. There is good reason for adopting this recommendation, as an adherence to the normal syntactical structure of English should guarantee a partial conceptual closure in the logical argument of the content. Alternatively, an extension of this reasoning also suggested that if each section in an article was shorter than 24 lines, then several short paragraphs could be displayed on the screen with the greater conceptual closure of the section (Shackel, 1983).

The lack of typographic cues and facilities for easy skimming and scanning, and the limited VDU screen size of 24 lines causing a typical printed journal page to take 2 to 2½ screen frames, mean that even when the structure is designed so that readers may access sections of the text, they would still not know where to locate sections of interest. The particular initial solution to this was to collect together all the major headings and figures into a contents list to be placed at a fixed point near the start of the structured article. The reader then always has the strategy of knowing where the contents list is placed and looking at it for direction to other parts of the text.

Thus the basic decision for the structure of an article was to place into the first four Entry slots the title, contents, summary and introduction respectively, followed by the main body of the article. At the end there were to be the references and the author's full address. This structure can clearly be seen from the example given in the *LINC Manual* (Shackel, 1983) (Figure 15).

Computer Human Factors Number 2 1983 Paper 10 Rec'd 1 May '83

Computers and People
by
A. Smith
Department of People, Computer University.

(2) CONTENTS OF THE PAPER	Entry Nos.
(3) Summary	3
(4) Introduction	4
(5) Background	5–7
(6) Methods — Equipment	8–10
(7) Methods — Subjects	11–13
Fig.1 Data of Subjects Sample	13
(8) Methods — Procedure	14–19
(9) Methods — Statistical Analysis	20–22
(10) Results — Data	23–26
Fig.2 Performance Times Data	24
Fig.3 Performance Errors Data	25
(11) Results — Analysis	27–33
Fig.4 Performance Times Graph Plot	28
(12) Discussion	34–40
(13) Conclusions	41–44
(14) Acknowledgements	45
(15) References	46–47
(16) Full Address	48

(3) SUMMARY

3 The problem of...
....

(4) INTRODUCTION

4 As a result of...
....

Figure 15. The Structure of the Start of an Article in the *Computer Human Factors* Journal

The figure shows similarities to the traditional presentation of a contents list as found in many books, with the set of numbers on the right corresponding to the screen 'pages' instead of the printed pages. We will return later in the chapter to a discussion of the use of the several numbering systems evident here.

3.1.4 References and Figures

Using paper there is a minimum of two strategies for handling pointers in the text to references and diagrams and many ways of presenting these pointers. For example, some journals use footnotes with the text marked with numbered superscripts; another use of numbers is in an ordered sequence of references numbered at the end of the article and marked in the text as superscripts (e.g. *Scholarly Communication*) or as a number of square brackets (e.g. *The Computer Journal*); another (and by now the most common in the field) is to have an alphabetic list of references at the end of the article and the text marked with the author and year of publication with an additional lower case letter when the year proves insufficient identification. The latter was adopted for the *Computer Human Factors* journal.

A similar variety exists for figures, diagrams and tables, although by far the most frequent is to have a dual sequential numbering system of such addenda to the text and to call them figures and tables. The text is then marked with a reference to the figure or table, for example '(see Figure 4)'. The lack of typographic cues to distinguish the different nature of the text also posed a problem which was resolved by a set cue of dashed double lines on each side of the figure itself.

Nowhere, however, were seen more clearly the limitations of an enforced linear structure and a relatively slow display speed than in pointing to the references and figures in this way.

Consider the task of the reader when a reference is found marked in the text:

1. Note reference in mind.

2. Display contents list to note where Reference Section may be found

3. Display reference list.

4. Return to section of text.

Putting aside, for a moment, the complex nature of the commands necessitated by the early versions of the software in these circumstances, it will be readily apparent that the memory load is high, that both the reference and the section of text have to be remembered accurately. Consider the difference between this and using the well-known 'keeping a finger in the page' strategy with printed pages where the reader can flick between two sections of text.

This provided the stimulus for development of the software in order to enable the reader to move freely around the article and consequently alter the markers in the article to facilitate reference to other parts of the text.

This development of the software is described in Section 2 and elsewhere (Pullinger, 1984b; Maude & Pullinger, 1984) and it is sufficient here to note the facilities:

— to step forwards and backwards in the text;

— to jump to any numbered entry containing text;

— to return to the previously displayed section of the text;

— to string search on first lines of entries to enable jumping to named section headings.

A change of the pointer in the text to include the Entry number in which the reference or figure is to be found, the use of a single entry for each reference and the command to return to the text previously displayed reduce the searching and memory load on the reader considerably. Thus each reference now appears as, for example, '(Pullinger 1984 [E37])', and each figure as '(see Figure 4 [E12])'. The task for the reader has now been reduced to:

1. see reference of interest;

2. type number to display reference;

3. type B for Back to return to reading place.

This change can now be seen to be a combination of two pointing strategies, numbering and the author and year of publication. The latter has been maintained for its inherent additional information given to the reader.

3.1.5 Developments

No assumption is made in this description of the design of the *Computer Human Factors* journal that the product is anything but an initial mounting of conventional paper structures on to electronic media whether it is appropriate to do so or not. Indeed, at the start of the project it was decided to replicate the traditional journal and article structure, so that authors, referees and readers need only learn how to use the electronic medium before introducing other changes (Pullinger et al, 1982, p 13). Thus the process of design and aspects that have needed to change are pointers to future designs of electronic journals and articles.

There are some aspects of change from the original design that have not previously been mentioned and which may be found in the following list together with those described above:

1. development of software with which to read articles;

2. change of pointers to include Entry number for all cross-referencing;

3. several short paragraphs put together in one Entry;

4. dropping section numbering leaving only Entry numbering;

5. greater use of headings in the middle of sections;

6. better display facilities for both VDU screens and printers.

The design of many VDU screens for reading text is far from satisfactory (Muter et al, 1982; Waern & Rollenhagen, 1983) and readers commented that they preferred short paragraphs broken by empty lines to be displayed on the screen. Thus, in general, articles are now structured so that as many paragraphs as will fit in a screen of 22 lines are concatenated. (The limit of an Entry was reduced from 24 lines to 22 lines by the use of the READ program.)

The dual numbering of both the sequence of sections in an article (marked by digits in parentheses in Figure 15) and the sequence of Entries/paragraphs (marked by digits embedded at the start of each entry following any heading) proved to be confusing for the reader. The dual numbering system replicated that found in printed journals which sometimes refer the reader both to numbered sections and to page number where appropriate. In the electronic medium, the situation is different because a reference to a section is insufficient for the reader to find quickly the relevant part by skimming and scanning. In this situation the reader needs a mechanism for being pointed to a particular screen of text — as has already been illustrated with references. The overt numbering of Entries was also needed for the implementation of the READ program to facilitate general movement around the article. Thus the section numbering was dropped. In its place is suggested a better use of headings to compensate for the loss of cues to the section structure of the text. The use of headings is similar to that in magazine and newspaper articles. Readers have commented that they liked the greater frequency of headings because these both provide structure through the text and highlight the content of the text.

Finally, we must not presume that readers use only a VDU screen. Many of the LINC started with printing terminals, some of them portable, some large teletypewriters, and some high-quality communicating printers (e.g. the Diablo daisywheel type). The software also permits printout in standard computer page size with automatic page numbering and a running header either set by the prospective reader or by default a shortened article title.

The electronic medium permits many new developments which include letters to the editor, which are included in the same 'issue', and discussion areas about each paper (see Figure 13). The most radical is in terms of the structure. This need not be linear and might involve a hierarchical structure with gradually increasing amounts of information (see Line, 1981; Hills, Hull & Pullinger, 1983) or a flexible modular structure allowing free browsing (for example, Reynolds, 1983). Other types of structure such as a matrix of sections are possible but have not yet been tried.

Conclusion

Just as a standard form has to some extent been developed in scholarly publishing to enable readers to use the journals more effectively and authors to write for them, so one might expect a similar form to develop in electronic journals. This cannot be expected without a considerable number of attempts at different structures by readers familiar with electronic media to discover the most useful designs. We hope that the description given here will add a little to the process of deriving an electronic journal structure that is easy to use and contributes to the passing of scholarly information between researchers and to information users.

3.2 The Development of the *References, Abstracts and Annotations Journal* (RAAJ)

On 1 May 1983, the BLEND experimental programme on electronic journals started the on-line *References, Abstracts and Annotations Journal*. This contains a database of bibliographic references in the subject area of Computer Human Factors up to 1981 and more recent references and authors' abstracts from selected journals. It is hoped that evaluative (or critical) annotations will be appended to these by members of the LINC using the BLEND system.

This section describes the design and some details of the RAAJ, together with the background considerations that led to the particular structure and format chosen.

The field of Computer Human Factors covers the development and design of hardware and software to make systems more usable, the interaction between computer-based systems, people and organisations and also the psychological attitudes and responses of users to systems. It has already grown large enough to justify an Abstracts Journal. This study explores the use of traditional procedures in selecting articles to which to make reference, followed by the provision of abstracts and the use of electronic 'messaging' to make annotations to the abstracts, possibly by several different readers. In this way it is expected to provide a more valuable form of Abstracts Journal.

Despite their apparent usefulness, abstracts journals are in general not well-used (Grogan, 1982) and one must ask whence scientists gather the information that leads them to articles of interest and importance. In many instances the recommendations of colleagues are an important part of this, supplemented by browsing through a regular group of journals taken either personally or by the institution library.

It seems, therefore, that extending an Abstracts Journal to include annotations and rapid provision of a core group of references and abstracts from regularly accessed journals might increase the use of this type of journal. This study started by setting up such a journal with a background database of references, many with annotations, and then putting in a core group of abstracts from regularly accessed journals as determined by a citation count in review papers. Evaluation of the process, of the iterative development, and of use are to be done as an integral part of the BLEND programme.

Background

1. References, Abstracts and Annotations

The RAAJ is being developed as a journal containing references, authors' abstracts and annotations to Computer Human Factors literature. Each entry in this journal aims to provide a full bibliographic reference, the authors' abstract and a critical summary of the paper. References, abstracts and annotations are not always all available for a particular entry, and where this is the case the information that is available will be entered.

The purposes of conventional (printed) abstracts journals are to direct people to the primary literature in a given field and to help the user locate the original text. Primary literature includes books, monographs, primary journals, reports, government documents, patents, conference papers, and pre-prints. Information provided by the secondary service may consist of tables of contents or bibliographic references arranged under an alphabetic or classified subject arrangement (Keenan, 1980) issued as printed bulletins and journals, cards, microforms, or on machine-readable tape.

The RAAJ will provide two types of information, factual (references and abstracts or summaries) and evaluative (annotations).

Bibliographic References

References give the authors' names and initials, the year of publication, the full title of the paper or book and information as to where to find it, e.g. the journal or publisher, volume and page numbers.

Authors' Abstracts

Abstracts are also informative, being factual descriptions or summaries of the content of an article provided by the author(s) and taken from the original document. Where authors' abstracts are not available, annotations can act as summaries of content as well as evaluations. These are often also referred to as abstracts, but in this report, describing this journal, the word 'abstract' will always refer to the authors' abstract.

Annotations

An annotation is an evaluative or critical comment or 'note' intended to be written by BLEND users, and appended to the reference and abstract. Annotations are intended to provide a value judgement or summary of the contents of the original documents for the benefit of other journal readers.

As with abstracts the word 'annotation' has come to mean different things in different fields, and its more general sense has been redefined from that of 'attaching a note' to, for example referring to a one or two sentence amplification of the title by information scientists. To clarify the difference between these one or two sentence amplifications and a longer comment, the latter are sometimes called evaluative or critical abstracts by this group of workers. Since the BLEND journal is concerned with the *process* of appending notes which may be of any length and either consist of a comment upon the content or an evaluation of it, it was decided to use the word 'annotation'.

Research into the provision of these different types of information about articles, reports and books can help us to understand the pattern of information use and scientific information flow more fully. It can, for example, help to throw light on two basic issues which have implications for the setting up of an appropriate service:

Firstly, researchers use different types of information in different ways, and these need to be identified in order to match the service provided to the needs of its users.

Secondly, many user studies reveal that the use of printed abstracting and indexing services in science and technology is low, and that there is a considerable neglect of many forms of unpublished source material (such as theses literature) as a vehicle for the dissemination of research results by librarians and by scientists and technologists themselves. For example, Slater & Fisher, 1969, found the most used documents in technical libraries were textbooks (50%), whereas periodicals were used by 43% and abstract journals and indexes by 22%; these figures are however very general ones. Grogan, 1982, p 207, mentions a more specific study on obtaining source material with only 7% using abstracts, 40% using periodicals and 19% using textbooks.

Some of the reasons hypothesised for the low use of printed abstract services are:

1. there is a lack of centralisation and co-ordination between services covering different types of literature, leading to duplication, overlap and gaps in services;

2. the information expected by the searcher is not there;

3. information given is out of date or incomplete;

4. comprehensive manual searching of relevant abstract and index services is extremely tedious and the standard vocabulary used for searching varies between services;

5. lack of awareness by scientists of abstract and indexing services;

6. abstract and indexing (i.e. formal) services are not as effective as informal methods of getting information, and do not easily fit into the way in which scientists work.

Indeed, research studies have been carried out about the way(s) existing services are inappropriate and these can help to improve the match between information availability and its use by the scientific community. Back, 1972, suggests that the reliance of researchers upon journal articles and textbooks as their primary written sources of information indicates that on-line retrieval methods are best used to assist in comprehensive, retrospective searching for references. On the other hand informal sources and citations in relevant documents are more likely to be used in the first instance because usually only a few relevant references are required and informal sources of information involve less effort by the users.

The RAAJ, taking into account some of the above hypotheses, might provide a better service because:

1. the literature in the field of Computer Human Factors and references to it are widely scattered among several disciplines. The gathering together of such references might aid researchers in obtaining their information;

2. the use of an electronic medium should result in information being up-to-date and topical;

3. manual searching can be replaced by better information retrieval procedures, such as deeper indexing, use of words taken from the original document, authors' names, or negative searching;

4. the electronic medium permits decentralisation of the production process and provision of reference and abstract information by readers. It could therefore provide access to unpublished works including reports, theses and other peripheral literature not currently covered by traditional abstracting and indexing services;

5. the informal methods of obtaining information used by scientists might be enhanced by the communication facilities available on the BLEND system with the journal increasing opportunities for contact.

2. A Survey of a Research Group

Over the five months spanning October 1982 — February 1983 the members of the HUSAT (Human Sciences and Advanced Technology)

Research Group at Loughborough University of Technology were interviewed. The Group comprises a multi-disciplinary team working within the broad area of Computer Human Factors. Approximately 20 people were informally interviewed and 16 replies received to a questionnaire concerning their patterns of information use, and a brief outline of results is presented here.

It was found that the preferred pattern of information use was initially an 'informal' approach, which was then supplemented by more formal literature-searching methods. The preferred patterns of the HUSAT Research Group are presented below (Figure 16).

It should be noted that in some situations it may be difficult to distinguish between 'formal' and 'informal' methods of information gathering. One may, for example, use a library 'informally' to gain ideas for new work or write to a colleague requesting information in a quite 'formal' way.

Nevertheless, this distinction has been supported in the other studies. Back, 1972, for example, uses Zaltman's categorisation of sources of information: formal channels, semi-formal channels, and informal channels (Zaltman, 1968).

The summary of results for the HUSAT Research Group suggests that it might be beneficial to provide a computerised service to bridge the gap between formal and informal methods of obtaining relevant information by providing factual and evaluative information about references. Instead

---

Sources of 'Computer Human Factors'

      — no centralised information system or index
      — source materials scattered

Current and retrospective references obtained by:

Informal Methods	*Formal Methods*
— Personal contacts	— University library
— Personal collections	— Catalogues
— Departmental collections	— Key abstracting/indexing
— Browsing through current	services
journals	— Subject bibliographies
— Citations from books	— Inter-library loans
— Information bulletins	service
(or external agencies)	— Publishers' copies

Figure 16. Present Sources of Computer Human Factors Information as Derived from a Survey of the HUSAT Research Group

---

of consulting a colleague or series of printed abstract and indexing services in order to trace relevant items, one could speedily find out references available on a particular subject, for what applications they are suited, how clearly the information is presented, relevance to the desired purpose, and what other colleagues think of the references.

Informal methods seem to be popular with researchers because they deliver a few relevant references with the least amount of effort, even though they do not supply all the relevant ones. Formal sources may be capable of supplying all the relevant references, but at a considerable expenditure of effort. Thus for an on-line system to be widely accepted and used, Back, 1972, recommends that it must be designed so that the effort required to

Sources		*Studies*				
		1	2	3	4	5
1.	Formal Sources					
	a. Citation Service	58%	0%	43%	23%	7%
	b. Review or Bibliography	16%				
	c. Card Catalogues	10%		**	***	
2.	Semi-Formal Sources					
	a. Citations	80%				
	b. Publishers' Literature					19%
	c. Librarian	8%	0%			
	d. Conference Presentation					
	e. Advertisement					7%
3.	Informal Sources					
	a. Scanning Journals	77%	31%	39%*	48%	4%
	b. Reprint File		57%			
	c. Personal Index	47%		**	***	
	d. Conversation	66%	12%	9%	13%	41%
	e. Correspondence	31%				
	f. Document Distribution	26%				
	g. Meetings					
4.	Other Sources				12.4%	17%****

   *   Uncertain whether references obtained by scanning journals or searching reprint file.
  **   9% together.
 ***   6% together.
****   Including prior knowledge of book's production (11%).
      Study 1   Martyn (1964, p 17)
            2   Allen (1966, Section 4.14)
            3   Urquhart (1965, p 118)
            4   Wood & Bower (1969, p 155)
            5   The American Psychological Association (1965, Vol, 2, p 248)

Figure 17. Reference Sources Used (Back, 1972)

retrieve relevant references from the computer is not much greater than the effort expended using other methods.

Figure 17 summarises five studies reviewed by Back, 1972, and indicates the use made of different reference sources by researchers.

Given the ready accessibility of formal information sources, informal sources must therefore have distinct advantages over them to account for their use for a range of purposes. He suggests that the advantages of both formal and informal sources should be combined in the design of an on-line reference retrieval system.

Designing the RAAJ

1. Introduction

The background research and survey pointed to development areas for the journal and more information was sought in these areas to create the journal. In order to provide a service which brought together the scattered literature, it was necessary to develop a mechanism by which the boundaries of Computer Human Factors could be established. The development of a classification scheme was one such mechanism adopted and a survey undertaken of the HUSAT Research Group with comments from the LINC and other interested parties.

However, owing to the timescale, the initial content of the journal was based on providing a background annotated references database, irrespective of the classification scheme and of a citation count to establish journals from which to provide references and authors' abstracts.

A classification scheme is one way of organising material to give control over the language used as an aid to retrieval, by providing standard terms for use both in the indexing process and for interactive searches. Apart from the need to develop aids for browsing and retrieving information, the process of adding annotations on to recent references and authors' abstracts had to be established.

This section describes research and development in these areas which led to the creation of the RAAJ.

2. The Extent of Computer Human Factors – a Classification Survey

The first step in the development of a classification of the topic of Computer Human Factors was to consider existing classifications in the field to see to what extent these might meet the needs of the journal. The classifications studied included, for example, the classification of the University of Sheffield Biomedical Information Service abstracts on Man-Computer Interaction, the classification used in the *Ergonomics Abstracts* journal and a list of the major factors in man-computer interaction suggested by Shackel, (1979, in Shackel, 1981b).

All of these existing classifications cover aspects of man-computer interaction, but few are comprehensive. A first draft of a possible classification system was therefore drawn up based on a composite of the relevant parts of existing classifications, and this was circulated to approximately 20 members of the HUSAT Research Group for their comments. They were asked to comment on the comprehensiveness of the classification, its appropriateness to their field of work, and were asked wherever possible to add synonyms or alternative headings, so that the terms used in the classification would cover all those in current use in the field.

Feedback from this exercise was used to compile a second draft classification which was again circulated for comment to the same members of the Research Group, and was also published in *INTERACT* (the newsletter of IFIP Working Group WG 6.3) and on the BLEND system for readers to comment upon.

In order to assess the practical usefulness of the classification, members of the HUSAT Research Group were given a list of 32 titles of recently published papers on topics covered by the heading 'Computer Human Factors', and were asked to assign these to one or more of the classification headings.

As a result, some further comments and suggestions have been put forward, which are being taken into account in the final development of the classification, currently in preparation.

3. Initial Content of the Journal

The survey of the HUSAT Research Group and suggestions made by the LINC indicated the need to gather together references widely scattered in the literature. Further, they suggested the requirement for a database of references of past material, as well as gathering new references from current journals.

The database of past material was generated by taking the references and annotated bibliographies of some review papers published over the past five years:

Eason, 1979, Man-computer Communication in Public and Private Computing.
Gibson, 1979, An Annotated Bibliography of Man-computer Communication.
Ramsey & Atwood, 1979, *Human Factors in Computer Systems: a Review of the Literature.*
Miller & Thomas, 1977, Behavioural Issues in the Use of Interactive Systems.
Shackel, 1981, The Concept of Usability.

Current awareness is to be maintained by gathering references and authors' abstracts from journals dated January 1982 and onwards. After analysing possible working patterns of researchers it was decided to keep the major sections of past material and current journals separate for two reasons:

1. Readers may not wish to look at abstracts on-line for current awareness for which they receive hard-copy journals through the post or which they regularly access in the library.

2. Readers may know what they receive or have in the library so that they can annotate these more easily than others.

Seven journals were selected on a frequency count of reference lists in some major recent review papers (including the five noted above). These are:

>   *Applied Ergonomics*
>   *Behaviour and Information Technology*
>   *Ergonomics*
>   *Human Factors*
>   *IEE Transactions, Systems, Man & Cybernetics*
>   *International Journal of Man-Machine Studies* (IJMMS)
>   *Journal of Applied Psychology*

The content of the journal will include all relevant titles and abstracts from these journals and also from 31 other identified journals which are peripheral to the subject area but which may contain articles of interest.

The structure of the BLEND system lends itself well to the separation of these categories as suggested above (see Figure 18).

Project: References, Abstracts and Annotations Journal.

Activities:
1. Database of references up to about 1980 as devised from the five bibliographies.

2.	Applied Ergonomics	References and Abstracts from January 1982					
3.	Behaviour and Information Technology	,,	,,	,,	,,	,,	,,
4.	Ergonomics	,,	,,	,,	,,	,,	,,
5.	Human Factors	,,	,,	,,	,,	,,	,,
6.	IEE Transactions, Systems, Man and Cybernetics	,,	,,	,,	,,	,,	,,
7.	IJMMS	,,	,,	,,	,,	,,	,,
8.	Journal of Applied Psychology	,,	,,	,,	,,	,,	,,
9.	Other journals	,,	,,	,,	,,	,,	,,

Figure 18. The Project and Activity Structure of RAAJ

4. The Process of Browsing, Retrieving Information and Annotating

The exact way in which researchers would use the journal, or the different purposes for which they might use it, are not known until research can be done. The development process starts by creating procedures which are as near to what is required as possible. In order to aid this development, the survey of the HUSAT Research Group also examined the different user aspects required by members for an internal database retrieval system. A summary of these is given in Figure 19. Asterisks show where a feature was considered to be a minimum requirement of an information retrieval system. Brackets indicate additional requirements suggested by HUSAT staff.

Browsing

These speculated requirements suggested various software aids for readers of the journal. In conjunction with Mr. Tim Maude of the University of Birmingham, and within the time and resource constraints of the BLEND experimental programme, a software program was developed through two prototypes (Maude & Dodd, 1983). This program is called BROWSE and permits browsing the database by, for example, stepping through the references or by giving fairly vague access words. BROWSE is also designed for single-character string searching for retrieval of a specified range of items, but at present does not provide sophisticated retrieval facilities as these are developed and are already in use on service systems.

	% of Respondents

1. *GENERAL USER REQUIREMENTS*
   (Accessible) (e.g. terminals easily available to all)
   (Reliable)
   *Comprehensive   36
   *Fast   21
   *Accurate   29
   *Up-to-date   36
   (Secure)
   (Easy-to-use)

2. *FLEXIBILITY*
   Forms of output (a) and ways of accessing information (b) should
   be both flexible and allow discretion by the user.
   a) *Output*
   Full text   21
   *Accurate bibliographical ref. only   50
   Full reference   71
   i.e. recall or print combinations of the following:
   *Abstracts   71
   Citations   36
   Annotations   36
   Location   71
   Status (confidential/open access)   71
   *Availability   71
   *Keywords Used   71

   b) *Access to a Reference*
   Users would like to be able to retrieve on any or all of
   these characteristics, singly or in combination.
   Multi-access   64
   *Keywords (key concepts)   21
   *Author   21
   *Title   14
   Year   14
   Journal title   14
   *Browsing/scanning capability on hard or soft copy   58

3. *RELEVANT TO THE TASKS OF USERS* (Task Match)
   Users must have the flexibility to group materials to their own
   specific requirements by grouping related items together, i.e.
   by:
   *Author   42
   *Subject   64
   *Project   50
   (Date)

4. *AIMS OF THE SYSTEM*
   1. To avoid duplication of material and effort and
      increase access to material already held.   36
   2. To produce accurate references for report writing.   58
   3. To provide lists of all references on a particular
      topic, by a particular author, or related to a
      particular project.   71
      This problem-solving approach was considered to be
      very important.

Figure 19. User Requirement Summary

Retrieving Information

Access to references, author abstracts and annotations needs to be flexible to take account of variations in the amount of information which users have available to conduct their search, i.e. browsing might involve searching on vague criteria, whereas the search for a specific item can be led by use of, for example, author name.

This suggests that multiple access points are necessary, e.g. retrieval by keyword and by data field:

Keywords:

> word strings taken from title or abstract of original documents. Usually indicating subject content of a document.

Data field:

> fixed format information such as:
> author name
> annotator's name/institute
> book details
> date of annotation
> entry number

Annotating the references and authors' abstracts

The use of an electronic communication medium as a basis for the journal allows readers to make comments on any reference that is familiar to them or which they read as a result of browsing or searching the journal. Indeed the main aim of the creation of this journal on the BLEND system is to explore the feasibility and use of such an annotating facility.

The use of informal recommendation of the worth of articles or books for particular purposes has already been noted above. The value of the recommendation itself depends on the perceived knowledge and authority of the recommender. Thus at the face-to-face meeting of the Computer Human Factors researchers using the BLEND system (LINC), it was recommended that retrieval should also be possible by the name of the annotator. There were two possibilities for the process of annotation, to allow readers to append comments themselves or to use a sub-editor to append the comments. The advantages of the former include immediacy of the comment, whereas the disadvantages include the need for a greater sophistication of editing facilities and an automatic generation of access words including the annotator's name. For the start of the journal, therefore, a sub-editor will be responsible for the collecting, checking of spelling and accuracy and submission of the annotations. The annotators will send their contributions as Notes (electronic mail messages) to the sub-editor.

Conclusion

We have discussed the background to the creation of an Abstracts Journal for Computer Human Factors and, in viewing the research on the use of such journals, propose to avoid some of the problems experienced hitherto. The most important of these seems to be the lack of use of abstracts journals and the preferred pattern of informal contact in order to get a few relevant references even if an exclusive covering of a particular area is not made.

The implications that have been drawn from the studies and the surveys of the HUSAT Research Group have led to:

1. a separation of the database into current journals and a large database of past material;

2. a flexible software aid for browsing and searching, though not a sophisticated search tool;

3. the possibility of annotating references to guide others as to their content and value.

These have been implemented in the BLEND system with as near a best guess at good design as possible, accepting limitations both on the system and on resources as to sophistication of the design. Doubtless, the design will prove insufficient in places, but it is hoped that the use, comments and suggestions by the LINC will lead to an iterative development of a journal that will be found useful.

4 COMMUNITIES OF USERS ON THE BLEND SYSTEM

4.1 The Setting Up of Other Communities

Under the plans drawn up and accepted by BLR&DD, there was provision for five to six communities to use the BLEND system during the programme. The purpose of this was to explore the type, range and subject matter of communication in order to see how these and other factors affected the messaging in a community. Thus there were a number of requirements of each community.

1. Under the terms of the contract between Infomedia and the University of Birmingham, the people must form a distinct group — i.e. one must easily be able to determine the membership qualification.

2. Also under the terms of the contract any commercial use is excluded.

3. Any proposed use must be new or a novel use of electronic communication media. There are commercial services already available for electronic mail and messaging.

4. Excepting the initial community which was to be funded by the BLR&DD, the communities must generally provide some form of additional funding independently of that given by user support and computer maintenance already established by the BLEND project management team.

Out of many initial approaches and discussions, there are now seven different sets of users:

LINC

The Loughborough Information Network Community was the first to be created in the programme by Professor Brian Shackel, the Project Director. It is composed of experts in the field of Computer Human Factors. Their range of communication spans from the formal level — in Refereed Papers — to the informal (Chit-Chat).

Students in Tele-Learning

Students at the University of Birmingham have been using the software in an experimental way for tele-learning, under the supervision of Dr. Peter Dodd. In particular, the NOTEPAD software on which BLEND is based allows one to stay in a communication mode while running programs (see Dodd, 1982).

MACE

MACE is the West Midlands Regional Office of the Microelectronics in Education Programme. This community wished to put its newsletter on the BLEND system, and also to transfer programs easily between local teachers' centres.

Library Schools

Most of the library schools in Britain are Readers of the LINC journals, in order to experience and consider what the future may hold for libraries. This community will be writing papers based on its experience, and contributing ideas about information storage and retrieval aspects.

FERN

The Further Education Research Network started trials in September 1983, and is concerned with, in the first instance, communication through a cumulative newsletter, allowing participation by all readers.

BIOTECH

A consortium in the South of England is in need of a cumulative database for research and communication in its field of work. It started trials on the BLEND system in December 1983.

Alvey News

In the Alvey initiative by the British government one of the sections, headed by Mr. D.L.A. Barber, is Infrastructure and Communication. The development of a proper national data communication network requires experience of many different systems. Thus an invitation was extended to those associated with Alvey to use the BLEND system. This started in February 1984.

The communities are now described in fuller detail, excepting LINC and the students, in a structured format on the following pages. The LINC is described in detail in the following chapter.

Community name: MACE

Background and nature of the community

MACE is the West Midlands Regional Centre for Microelectronics and Computers in Education, an information centre funded by the government as part of the national Microelectronics Education Programme started in 1980. The country has been divided into 14 regions for the purposes of the MEP, each region having a Regional Information Centre. The MACE Regional Centre forms the information unit for the West Midlands.

The main purpose is to set up an information network within the region to serve all 11 constituent local education authorities. The MACE centre has three main functions:

— the provision of an information service;

— to assist in the training of teachers in all aspects of computing and its applications;

— curriculum development.

Interaction on the BLEND system

The initial aim of the project is to use the BLEND system to publish one newsletter and one magazine per term and also to have the following forms of communication: messages; program lists and file transfer facilities to permit the rapid exchange of programs.

Funding

Other than the infrastructure support for BLEND and the evaluation work funded by BLR&DD, no explicit funding was needed since most centres had equipment and telephone lines already operational.

Progress so far

Stage 1 (June/July 1983) — The newsletter was set up. Wendy Olphert interviewed all members concerning their access to the system and their expectations of the system; she also conducted a non-participative observation of naive log-ins.

Stage 2 (August 1983) — Non-participative observation on use of BLEND.

Stage 3 (February 1984) — Follow-up interviews to find out 'what has happened'.

References

OLPHERT W. Report on the Preliminary Evaluation of the MACE Community — July 1982. HUSAT Memo. No. 265 R.

Community name: LIBRARY READERS

Background and nature of the community

Several of the library schools throughout the UK requested access to the only experimental electronic journal in order to demonstrate to students the possibilities of the future.

Interaction on the BLEND system

The purpose of the project is to obtain data relating to the way users read material on screens. The material to be accessed includes the journal, *Computer Human Factors* (CHF), the bulletin and the newsletter *LINC News*. One set of modifications made to the NOTEPAD software over the last two years has been in the area of providing aids to reading text on screens. Clearly the project team wishes to gain feedback into the effectiveness of these modifications. The BLEND project embraces all levels of communication from the formal to the informal. This project is focussing upon a consideration of the formal levels and particularly upon the readership status.

Funding

All the library schools have terminals for access to other databases so the BLR&DD has provided a certain allowance for telephone expenditure for each institution.

Progress so far

Many library schools have logged into BLEND for demonstration in their teaching schedule. Some have encouraged students to try out novel features of the journals and City University has run an experiment on naive use of BLEND (Bernard, 1983).

Community name: FERN

Background and nature of the community

A short summary taken from its literature reads:

THE FERN PROJECT

The Further Education Research Network is an independent, self-financing charity, established and organised by teachers seeking to equip themselves with the knowledge and techniques relevant to contemporary developments. Membership is available to all teachers in further and higher education and the organisation is administered by an annually elected executive committee.

FERN's aims may be summarised as follows:

1. to make it possible for teachers to identify the most effective support which they and their students can receive from industrial and commercial concerns, research agencies, centres of teacher training, local authorities and central government organisations;

2. to provide members with the opportunity to extend their professional abilities and experience by helping them contribute to research and course evaluation exercises undertaken by other educational organisations;

3. to encourage and support a wide variety of investigations initiated by members which may increase student learning performance; current projects include the development of new computer aïded learning materials, and the analysis and evaluation of classroom interaction using traditional teaching techniques;

4. to organise workshops, seminars and conferences so that members involved in research studies, or the development of new teaching materials, can gain a wider circulation for their ideas, and be stimulated by the views of their colleagues;

5. to promote the responsible examination and discussion of educational issues and encourage members to demonstrate their continuing professional development by publishing a periodical and occasional research papers.

An effective communication system is essential for the aims of the organisation to be achieved. FERN was founded in 1979; within four years it was clear that the very success of the network threatened to limit its effective operation using traditional administrative systems and techniques.

1. A central office, even when highly efficient, could not collect and distribute ideas and information quickly enough to keep pace with the needs of a growing number of teachers and the increasing scale and variety of their research activities.

2. In further education, there are no established expectations which support the practice and publication of action research. Ensuring informal discussions between teachers is an essential step in developing a tradition of enquiry and investigative study.

3. A traditional administrative structure can act as a disincentive, by reducing direct and immediate contact between teachers seeking to discuss issues of common concern.

4. The opportunity for members to meet at familiar types of conferences or workshops is limited owing to the inability of colleges to release colleagues from teaching responsibilities for extended teaching and course evaluation studies.

Interaction on the BLEND system

In drawing up the specifications needed in communications in the above considerations, the organiser of FERN, Mr. David Rogers, learnt of the

BLEND system. After a period of negotiation it was possible to map all the identified requirements on to the BLEND system. Thus, in the use of messaging, conferencing, newsletters and journal, there is an interesting experimental study in the provision of a medium for an already identified set of requirements.

Funding

The FERN-associated colleges of further education have agreed to spend appropriate money so that members have equipment. The BLEND project grant from BLR&DD is supplying FERN Centre with a TORCH microcomputer and printer.

Progress so far

Technical specification of equipment to enhance existing BBC micros. Test Project set up September 1983.

References

OLPHERT W. & PULLINGER D.J. The BLEND System: FERN strategy document. HUSAT Memo. No. 300 R.

Community name: BIOTECH

Background and nature of the community

The establishment of the BIOTECH Community is centred upon the Institute of Biotechnological Studies (IBS) and is administered from the Polytechnic of Central London.

Three major groupings of users are identified at:

— The Polytechnic of Central London (PCL).

— University College, London (UCL).

— The University of Kent at Canterbury (UKC).

IBS is the sole educational grouping recognised by the Department of Trade and Industry for support in its Biotechnology and Industry programme. IBS has been accepted as the principal biotechnology centre in the UK for the training of scientists from developing countries in relation to the International Programme on Biotechnology.

Interaction with the BLEND system

The aim of the establishment of the BIOTECH Community on the BLEND system is to further the development of efficient techniques and methodologies for the transfer of biotechnological information. The activities envisaged by the community include messaging, teleconferencing, preparation of a newsletter containing information on training opportunities in biotechnology and the preparation and editing of reports singly and jointly. It is also intended to provide experience in the use of home-based workstations.

Funding

To allow purchase of terminal equipment and installation of telephone lines, PCL received a grant from BLR&DD.

Progress so far

Phase 1. Setting up trial Project on the BLEND system August 1983.

Phase 2. Setting up single Project and supply of first manual January 1984.

References

WEBB T. & PULLINGER D.J. BIOTECH Strategy Document. HUSAT Memo. No. 301 R.

Community name: Alvey News

Background and nature of the community

The report of the Alvey Committee entitled *A Programme for Advanced Information Technology* was published in 1982. In order to implement the recommendations of this report, the government has now set up the **Alvey** Directorate under the leadership of Brian Oakley. The Alvey Programme is a collaborative research programme for the UK. It will be run as a matrix of technologies and major projects taking advantage of technological developments. A plan of action will be drawn up for each of the four main technologies making up the Programme:— Very Large Scale Integration, Software Engineering, Intelligent Knowledge-Based Systems and Man-Machine Interface. These plans will be drawn up by working parties consisting of experts and the academic community. Although not specifically identified as such in the original report, the Infrastructure and Communications aspects are now regarded as sufficiently important to merit the status of a fifth area of activity, including research.

Interaction on the BLEND system

The purpose of the BLEND system being opened by invitation is to enable the Alvey Directorate and the British IT community to explore the potential of this type of system as a medium for messages, conferencing, news and information exchange.

Progress so far

Trial Project mounted in BLEND system. Invitation published.

References

An Introduction to the BLEND system entitled, 'BLEND Network and Electronic Journal Project' in *Alvey Newsletter* No. 2.

An invitation to join the BLEND system in *Alvey Newsletter* No. 3.

4.2 User Support

The problems of casual users have already been summarised elsewhere in this report (see Section 2). There we considered the need for a high consistency in the command structure to aid ease of use and the need for a conceptual consistency throughout the software system. However, the same argument applies to all the support for a user. Thus the observation that naive users bring no understanding with them to the system and make the best rational rule available to explain the system's behaviour, which will often be confounded, implies that rapid help in some form needs to be available. This should both inform as to the next action to be taken by the user and also teach a little more about the system. The problem with experienced users is that they frequently have substantial preconceived ideas and already have learned many command structures. To learn a new structure not often used (relative to other systems) would in any case impose a high memory load, but they have to cope with the frustration that they know exactly what they want to do with the system conceptually but do not know which commands to give to accomplish it. This implies that a rapid means of informing them of the command is needed without a long explanation.

The BLEND system therefore provides to communities:

1. upon request, a list of possible commands when any prompt is displayed on the screen;

2. an area where messages asking for Advice and Help can be left in the BLEND system;

3. a credit-card-sized reminder as to log-in and facilities available;

4. a users' guide and manual;

5. a telephone service to a 'local expert', followed by back-up services, with named individuals and responsibilities, at Loughborough University of Technology and the University of Birmingham. An answerphone at Loughborough guarantees a reply within one working day.

This provides a series of Help 'shells' around the user so that, although they may not be used, nevertheless the user should feel as if there is always help available. That this is the case was demonstrated by the satisfaction expressed by members in the six-month and 35-month surveys of the LINC (Section 5). A full analysis of the use made of the facilities provided will be presented in the final reports.

5 THE LINC IN THE FIRST THREE YEARS

5.1 The Proposed Topic

The topic proposed for this part of the BLEND programme may be succinctly entitled 'Computer Human Factors'.

This may be defined as 'the science and technology of man-computer communication'. The topic should be considered from both human and computer viewpoints; so this involves not merely the theory and measurement of human behaviour and performance in man-computer communication (MCC), but also the study of computer system characteristics and performance in relation to human designers and users. The aim of this subject is to understand the relationship between people and computer hardware and software during MCC, so as to optimise system efficiency and human satisfaction (the system here being the combined man-computer system).

The scope and current status of MCC has been surveyed in a recent state-of-the-art report (Shackel, 1979). Lest the topic should be considered too narrow to sustain a satisfactory range of electronic journals, its scope may be indicated by the breadth of the major factors listed in Figure 20.

In fact, it is suspected that the scope may prove to be too wide, as apparently was found to be the case for the USA project. This was first envisaged to be the 'measurement and theory of human performance in man-machine systems' (Prof. N. Moray's application to BLR&DD), but was established as 'the nature and measurement of mental workload' (letter to participants from Prof. T.B. Sheridan at the start of project, 8 August 1978).

5.2 The Proposed Procedure

A community of about 40 to 50 participants in Britain was assembled (all those listed in Appendix 7 are well-established workers in the human sciences or the computer and information-processing sciences). Each participant was told that he/she should have use of a suitable terminal through a telephone line, thus being able to access the host computer system. The software system would provide private working file sections for each

Human performance
Basic characteristics and limitations, e.g. size, speed, skills, errors, flexibility, etc.
Special aspects, e.g.   Selection.   e.g. Modelling the user.
                          Training.   Decision making.
                          User support.   Problem solving.

Computer system performance
Basic characteristics and limitations, e.g. capacity, speed, reliability, etc.
Special aspects for MCI, e.g.   Language facilities.
                                  System response time.
                                  Security.

Hardware interface
Displays, controls, terminals and consoles.
Applied ergonomics for good workstation design.
Human need and new devices.

Software interface
The non-hardware communication media.
Language and linguistic systems (MCI aspects).
Information organization;
    e.g. logical structure of content and procedures.
    e.g. message structure and verbosity, display format and layout (including, e.g.
    microfilm output, questionnaire and other input forms).

Environment
Physical: workstation space and layout, lighting, noise, etc.
Psychological: influence (e.g. via motivation, strain, etc.) of the working group, of
the job structure (e.g. shift working), of the system structure (e.g. open/closed,
rigid/flexible, etc.) of the social climate and of the organization design.
Applied ergonomics and social science for good environment design.

Specific applications, e.g.:
Specialist users.   Computer assisted learning.
Business users.   Computer aided design.
Naive users.   Man/computer telecommunications.
Public systems.   Computer conferencing.

Special problems, e.g.:
Evaluation: Especially criteria and methods.
              Especially social implications versus cash costs.
              Importance of real world studies (not in laboratory only)
Privacy of personal information.
Ergonomics of programming and the job of the programmer.
Documentation and related job aids.
Influence of MCI upon job design and organization design.
Influence of MCI upon society.

Figure 20. The Scope of Man-computer Communication (MCC)
(Figure 3 from Shackel, 1979)

participant, facilitate all communications (whether private or public)
between participants, editor, referees, etc., enable 'conferencing', and hold
'public' files of 'accepted papers' constituting the final 'journal volumes'.

Each participant undertook to submit at least one paper and one shorter note during each year of the three-year experimental programme, and to keep a log book of related activity and experience at the terminal. The expectancies and reactions of the participants in taking part in the experiment were planned to be measured before, during and after use of the system.

On submitting a paper the author participant notifies the editor through the system that the paper has been entered. The editor registers and acknowledges it and directs it to appropriate referees, who will become aware of this when they next access the system. Refereeing involves the transmission of messages either personally or anonymously over the network, between referees and author either directly or via the editor (different procedures will be examined). If the paper is formally accepted, it is transferred in final form to the 'accepted papers' archive file, indexed and abstracted, and then made available to all members of the LINC. Papers rejected will not be archived, but may stay in the author's private file to which other members of LINC may have access with his permission.

Several other possible uses of the system, directly following upon this process, suggest themselves and are being explored (such as 'Letters to the Editor', 'Comments and Discussion' following a paper as in edited conference proceedings, etc.) but the main thrust at the start of this project was to submit papers and gain experience of the characteristics and processes of an electronic journal in the form of traditional refereed papers.

With regard to customary editorial and related procedures, most journals establish and develop guidelines and standard methods such as Notes for Contributors and Guidance to Referees. The standard procedures previously developed for the *Journal of Occupational Psychology* (by the Project Director) were rewritten *a priori* as seemed appropriate for an electronic refereed papers journal (in the LINC Members' Manual) and were revised and assessed during the programme.

5.3 The First LINC Meeting

The first face-to-face meeting of the LINC was held on 31 October 1980 at Loughborough University of Technology, and 42 out of a possible 51 persons attended. System manuals, training manuals and membership cards (with computer log-in passwords) were issued. Trial use of the network began on 15 November 1980. The BLEND system was announced and available for full use from 15 January 1981.

There were four discussion sessions which have been recorded in the report of the meeting (Shackel and Preston, 1980). The 27 topics included clarification on the public image of the project, scope for development, the help facilities, organisation and management, and technical questions relating to the BLEND system.

Following the meeting a period ensued in which two main activities were pursued:— first, the trial use of the NOTEPAD software for all those members who had suitable terminals and telecommunications equipment; second, interviews with a sample of the members to discover their working habits and attitudes with respect to traditional journals. Both these might have had a major influence on the use of a BLEND-type system and so the participant-members were given a questionnaire and were visited by a researcher. The results from this survey are described here.

5.4 Initial Survey

The Present Publishing Process – Is it liked?

The group of scientists surveyed was asked to place a cross on a 10 cm line marked at each end with 'Like' and 'Dislike' to answer the question 'Do you like the present system of publishing in refereed paper journals?'. The median response of five showed their ambivalence in recognising the value of print and certain aspects of the publishing process. In particular refereeing of papers is seen as keeping the quality of the journals higher than they would otherwise be, while, on the other hand, there is almost a unanimous dislike of the slow publication process, specifically the delays due to slow refereeing. Other dislikes included the restrictions imposed on writing papers owing to rigid standards of presentation; the occasional arbitrary and unhelpful refereeing, without the possibility of recourse to the anonymous referee; and the difficulty of locating relevant material in the multiplicity of journals in the field. Figure 21 summarises the free comments made.

Publication Delays

Clearly the aspect of the process that most worries scientists is the delay in publication of papers. In order to establish where delays occurred, a comprehensive collection of data was made for two UK journals for all papers arriving during a two-year period (Pullinger, 1984a). One journal experienced a change of editor, which was taken into account as the entire

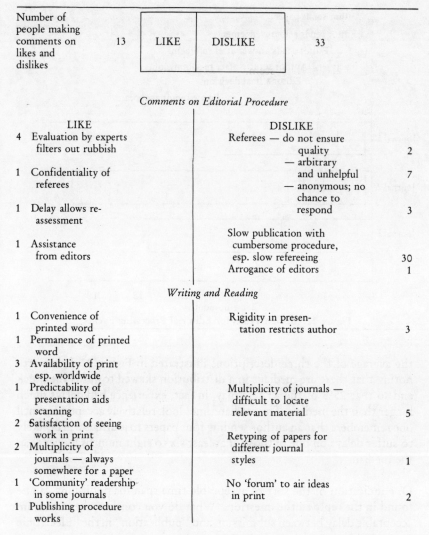

Number of people making comments on likes and dislikes	13	LIKE	DISLIKE	33

Comments on Editorial Procedure

LIKE		DISLIKE	
4	Evaluation by experts filters out rubbish	Referees — do not ensure quality	2
		— arbitrary and unhelpful	7
1	Confidentiality of referees	— anonymous; no chance to respond	3
1	Delay allows re-assessment		
1	Assistance from editors	Slow publication with cumbersome procedure, esp. slow refereeing	30
		Arrogance of editors	1

Writing and Reading

LIKE		DISLIKE	
1	Convenience of printed word	Rigidity in presentation restricts author	3
1	Permanence of printed word		
3	Availability of print esp. worldwide		
1	Predictability of presentation aids scanning	Multiplicity of journals — difficult to locate relevant material	5
2	Satisfaction of seeing work in print	Retyping of papers for different journal styles	1
2	Multiplicity of journals — always somewhere for a paper		
1	'Community' readership in some journals	No 'forum' to air ideas in print	2
1	Publishing procedure works		

Figure 21. Likes and Dislikes in Present Publishing Procedure of Refereed Papers

procedure was changed. Figure 22 summarises the median times in the publishing process from the author's viewpoint and shows that an average median is four months in refereeing and nine months in the printing queue (taking as a typical case a paper which is returned to the author once for editing prior to resubmission).

The median figures for editorial processing and publishing queues which are printed regularly in a number of US journals fall almost exactly around

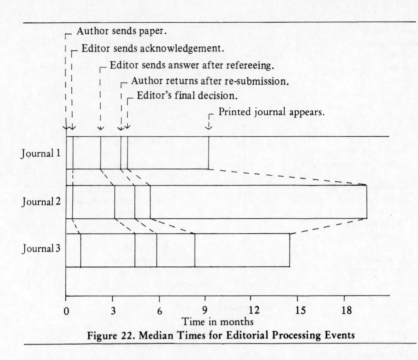

Author sends paper.

Editor sends acknowledgement.

Editor sends answer after refereeing.

Author returns after re-submission.

Editor's final decision.

Printed journal appears.

Journal 1

Journal 2

Journal 3

| 0 | 3 | 6 | 9 | 12 | 15 | 18 |

Time in months

Figure 22. Median Times for Editorial Processing Events

the average of the three descriptions illustrated in Figure 22. It is worth noting that these are medians in a distribution skewed towards the quick end so that 25% of the writers may, in fact, experience bad delays much longer than the median. The median times look relatively acceptable, until one remembers that an author sending four papers to journals will be likely to suffer delays on one of those of at least six to eight months longer than the median.

One indication of the sort of acceptable time span for publishing can be found in the reply to the question. 'What do you consider the maximum acceptable delay between submission and "publication" in the "Electronic Journal"?'. In an electronic journal there need be no printing queue if chosen, i.e. the papers can be published as soon as they have been accepted by the editor. Whatever policy is adopted by the editorial board in an electronic journal, since there need be no restrictions on the size of an 'issue', a paper would have only to wait until the next 'issue' to be published (if 'issues' are used). Thus the question implicitly seeks to find the maximum acceptable time period for initial editorial processing, to which the general reply is three months or under (see Figure 23). There is recognition by some respondents that if re-submission was involved, then a longer period may be acceptable.

There is another aspect to this delay which those wishing to participate in the information flow have noted; because of lengthy publication delays, only statements of work finished and accomplished appear. There is little possibility of discussion with the author on 'live' issues or the creation of new research ideas integral to that particular piece of work.

Communication Between Reader and Author

When this group of scientists read, they do not in general communicate with the author, but 19% ask for reprints from the author. As writers they report that they receive fewer requests for reprints now than hitherto, except from the Eastern European countries. The reason for this appears to be the use of photocopying machines, which the Eastern bloc does not possess in such abundance. However, some say that they do receive requests for other papers they may have written or be in the course of writing and remark wryly that these are often from US research students being lazy about their literature searches! The reduction in requests for reprints by researchers at an equivalent level of expertise and experience seems to remove one point of contact which might facilitate dialogue about work. The wish for a greater amount of communication was very clearly expressed in the group's anticipation that an electronic journal with communication facilities would (a) aid discussions with authors while important ideas are being formulated, (b) enable more detailed and technical information to be obtained from specific authors than is normally written up in journal papers and (c) encourage interaction and community spirit in a group of researchers (see Figure 24).

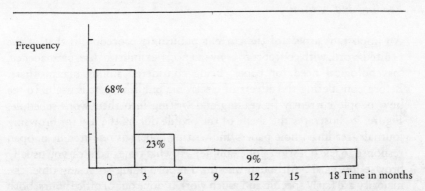

Figure 23. The Acceptable Maximum Length for Publication Delay in an Electronic Journal — a Histogram

It should, however, be remembered that these views are from a group of scientists engaged in work in the emerging field of Computer Human Factors. The members of this group may find themselves classified under many labels and research work published in many different journals. Consequently, they may have a greater need for identification with other members and for more detail of methodological and experimental techniques than might be necessary in more established subject areas.

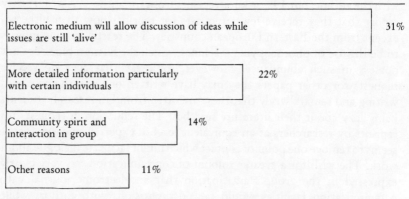

Figure 24. Percentages of the Total Number of People Interviewed who Gave Reasons for an Increased Exchange of Ideas in an Electronic Communication Network

Reading and Writing

An important aspect of the current publishing procedure is that of the printed word, with concepts of convenience, flexibility of use, permanence, 'psychological need for paper' being considered among many others. Before considering the effects of electronic publishing, it is useful to see how people currently fit reading and writing into their work schedule. Figure 25 illustrates the shape of the profile during the day for browsing journals, reading whole papers and writing papers as reported in an open response to the question (for example) 'At what time of day do you usually browse journals?'. Although one-third report doing so at any time, the majority are fairly specific and much work is done out of office hours, both when travelling and at home: 65% of browsing, 85% of reading whole papers and 63% of writing as reported by these scientists. Those interviewed were also asked how they approached a journal in order to read papers. Three strategies or purposes were adopted:

1. The general pattern of filtering through the stages — Title, Abstract, Results/Conclusions, References, Full text: possible photocopy.

2. A preliminary filter of Title and Abstract followed by a request for a photocopy for later reading.

3. Skimming through articles for new ideas without particular note of paper content.

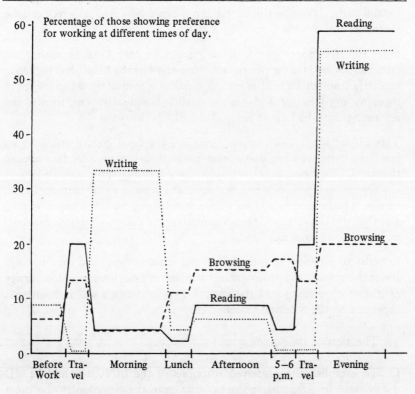

Figure 25. Times of Day for Reading, Browsing and Writing

It is to be noted that some senior and well-supported staff do not look at journals initially. Their awareness is maintained by having research staff, exclusive use of abstract journals or an information advisory service.

Lack of organisational support is particularly felt by researchers when it comes to writing. In the UK, although high respect is given to those who do research, there is little support in the way of secretarial staff or release from other duties. Thus most of those surveyed said that they would have liked to write more papers, and the lack of support may be illustrated by the fact that 51% typed first drafts themselves (either on typewriters or word-processors), 18% producing the finished product themselves. The rest used secretaries or typists but reported that the typing of papers is often given low priority relative to other tasks.

5.5 Six-Month Survey

The LINC started full trials on the BLEND system on 15 January 1981. Naturally, not all LINC members had obtained the necessary equipment for full participation by this date, but most members gradually received the terminals and modems.

Over the five-month period from January to May 1981, computer use statistics showed that approximately one-third of the LINC had logged in regularly (though with different frequencies), a second third had logged in regularly until Easter and hardly at all subsequently, and, finally, the remaining third had never entered the BLEND system.

Various facts were known that might have been contributory to an emerging pattern of decreasing use in the second third of users, for example that the DEC computer at the University of Birmingham was down 15% of the time from April to May 1981; another example was that many LINC members had experienced long delays in obtaining modem equipment etc.; and that the University Grants Committee cuts demanded both financial and discussion time sacrifices.

In order to establish how the LINC participants expressed their feelings about the system, the project team members at Loughborough University of Technology instigated the idea of a survey, which was unanimously approved by the Steering Committee.

The aims of the survey were:

1. To establish the perceived reactions of the LINC to the BLEND system, in particular to note what gave the community the most concern about its participation.

2. To discover any problems with which the project management team might help, in particular to linking hardware and software to facilitate communication.

3. To find out the extent to which each member participated in submitting one larger and one shorter paper per year to the BLEND system.

The Interview

Various survey techniques were considered, including written questionnaires sent through the postal system, questionnaires sent via the computer based message system in BLEND, telephone interviews and face-to-face interviews. Factors that influenced these considerations included the relative cost, the number of LINC members that would probably be contacted successfully by each technique, the availability of members' and the researcher's time.

In order to cover both those who had never and those who regularly logged into the BLEND system it was decided to hold a telephone survey. This survey presented structured questions while allowing free responses which were analysed subsequently.

The questions which were included in the interview covered five areas:

1. Use of the system
   — How much have you used the BLEND system?
   — Do you envisage this level increasing?

2. Hardware
   — Have you got all the equipment that you hoped for by now?
   — Access to equipment.

3. Design of system
   — What changes to the technical, software or procedural aspects of the BLEND system would you like to make?

4. User support
   — Have you found the user documentation satisfactory?
   — What other forms of user support would you like?

5. Scientific Communication — Have you had scientific communication through participation in this project with those with whom you did not previously communicate?
— Have you started a paper or dispatch for the project yet?

Discussion on Phone Survey

Attempts were made throughout June 1981 to contact each and every member of the LINC.

One hundred and thirty calls were made, 14 of which reached the person required on the first attempt and 36 of which were successful in the end. At the time of the survey there were 59 scientific LINC members so that the proportion of successful first time calls was 23.7% and the average number of calls made to each person 2.4.

It is to be noted that some were not tried for one of two reasons, either because they were contacted on the same phone call in the same location as another or the researcher was informed that another member was away on holiday or at a conference.

From an introductory questionnaire and interviews conducted in the first three months of the experimental programme, November 1980 — January 1981, the situation of most of the LINC members was known to the researcher. In this context it was decided not to make a set number of attempts to contact each person, but more attempts were made with those in a different situation from other members, in order to maximise the possibilities arising from the contact.

Although this was partially successful (see Figure 26) it is clear that the sample was largely determined by availability. As one would expect from such a sampling technique, views were biased more towards the users of the system, rather than the non-users, owing perhaps to their greater time availability in general.

General Response

The general response to being called by phone in this way was very positive in expression, although as one member quipped, 'Are you measuring us on a guilt scale?'. This latter point is reinforced by looking at the subject about which interviewees spent most time talking, which was noted on the

	0	SSFFFFFFF	
	1	SSSSSSSSSSSSSFFF	S = Successful contact made after
Number	2	SSSSSSSSSSFFFFFF	this number of calls
of	3	SSSSF	F = Failed to make contact after this
calls	4	SSSSF	number of calls
made	5	SSSF	
	6	F	Number of S = 36
	7	FF	Number of F = 24
	8	F	Total 60 (59 + 1 non-scientific)
	9	F	

Figure 26. Distribution of Successful and Unsuccessful Calls Made

occasion of the interview. Most time was spent by 17 interviewees on reasons why the BLEND system had not been used as much as they would have hoped. Most time was spent by nine on how they would change the system and by four on the need to establish a focal point of interest to users.

Discussion of Results

(1) Use of the BLEND System

The survey confirmed the impression given by the use pattern that many of the community had logged in a few times and, along with some of the regular users, had then not done so so frequently in the period from Easter to May 1981.

The reasons that were directly given in these explanations are presented in the following table. Each of them relates to problems of time and access inside a working-life with previously existing routines and demands. A discussion of the main areas follows the table.

(i) *Equipment* *People*

Access to equipment a problem	28
British Telecom delays	6
No equipment	1
(but note that nearly half had not got the equipment for which they had hoped)	
Difficulty logging through into DEC computer (BT + DEC)	6

(ii) *Time/Pressure*

Lack of time — LINC participation a low priority	13
Need deadlines towards which to work	2

(iii) *General*

At early stages not much return for investment of time	11
No natural reasons for use, system not integrated into normal work	3

Access

Access to equipment and from thence to the DEC at Birmingham formed one of the major problem areas:

1. delay in installation of lines and equipment by British Telecom;

2. political, bureaucratic non-co-operation and non-availability for installation of direct lines;

3. existing equipment and procedures not able to be extended to access Birmingham;

4. political, bureaucratic non-co-operation for terminals being in own rooms;

5. dislike for the conflict situation arising in finding others using terminals;

6. time constraints on when DEC may be accessed;

7. DEC not always running when accessed.

Six members reported lengthy delays in having telephone lines installed and awaiting modems to be delivered by British Telecom (then the Post Office). Other problems were caused by noisy lines for those using internal lines passing through switchboards or poor acoustic couplers. Although there is funding in the project with which to help participant members to come on-line by paying for installation of outside direct telephone lines to avoid switchboard line noise, this aid has been thwarted in several instances. The reasons are (a) political — 'why should so-and-so have an outside line not under supervisory control?', (b) problems of establishing a procedure for payment of bills, and (c) knowledge of five to six month waits for British Telecom to install or being told that there were 'no new numbers available in your area'.

The five to six month wait also applies for alteration to existing lines in the London area and hence terminals are not moved to more accessible rooms or to the office where a member works.

Only eight members have terminals in their office; 21 have access to terminals in another room in the same building whereas seven members had to walk to another building (where the terminal phone may well be under lock and key). Some of these members, moreover, have to walk to another building even though they may have a terminal sitting on their desks, which they regularly use. These members in computer departments have terminals connecting to their mainframe. If that mainframe can connect by some procedure to the telecommunications system or to a computer network linking with Birmingham, then the member may use his familiar procedures to access BLEND, e.g. through MIDNET. However it is possible that this is not the case, and it seems that members will not be inclined to walk and then use unfamiliar terminals and procedures that duplicate areas in which they may already have some experience, e.g. of ARPAnet or of SERCNET.

Offers of financial help in these last cases to install lines and make access easier have been refused in two cases. The members wished to use the systems with which they were familiar and preferred to seek ways of so doing rather than getting more equipment which was incompatible with their existing practices and which would not make their working life more convenient for the preparation of research papers, given the cost constraints in the availability of this help.

Specifically, for this type of member, computer or satellite networks need to be developed so that, when wanting a system on a particular computer, it is able to be accessed by a variety of channels according to the working procedures already in practice, which might include a filing system, knowledge of editor and other text-processing familiarity.

A number of reasons were given in the preliminary interview visits, which were also reported in the telephone survey, why it was not permissible for LINC members to move terminals to their own rooms. To list just a few:—

a terminal is seen as an extra piece of equipment which might not be consistent with an equalisation of status; a terminal, despite being bought for the experimental project, is seen as a departmental asset; all terminals are considered to have to be centrally located in one room to facilitate electric cable and table requirements.

When people go to a room in which a terminal is positioned and find another person engaged in work on the terminal, or external telephone line, conflict may arise. If the member wishes to go ahead and use the system then he/she has to interact, possibly unfavourably, with the existing user. Some members reported avoiding this situation completely rather than risk creating an unpleasant atmosphere.

Time-sharing is a constraint that may interact both with a working life and also with the time availability of the University of Birmingham DEC computer. At the time of the survey, this had been available for 24 hours a day during vacations but not available 10–12 a.m. and 2–4 p.m. during term time. Some users had experienced several attempts at log-in while the computer was down. During the period Easter — June 1981 the DEC was down 15% of the time. This figure would appear much higher to a user restricted to hours outside 10–12 a.m. and 2–4 p.m., when the engineers who work normal working hours would not be available to get the DEC operating again.

Members stated that their participation in the BLEND project was of lower priority than their other work. This was both a conscious decision, for example participation might not be what they are paid to do, and an unconscious one. In the latter case there are two contributory factors: firstly a highly reactive, rather than proactive, response to the demands of the moment. This seems to be true particularly for university members who generally have inadequate secretarial and clerical support. This is further exacerbated by a lack of visibility of participation, for example a member might well answer the letter that has been hanging around the in-tray for three weeks, whereas he/she would not log into a terminal in another room (owing to the lack of the visible cue to the need for action.)

Some members said that as yet they do not find any 'natural' reasons for using the system. This may well be due to the returns as they are perceived in the first five months of the experiment. Information, papers, bibliographies etc. are relatively limited. Unlike databases, no information of a scientific content was placed in the system and consequently members felt that, for their investment of time in learning the procedures and searching, there is little return.

(2) Design of the BLEND system

The members of the LINC who were surveyed made 53 suggestions about the changes they would like to see made. Sixteen of these related to the ease of accessing the DEC computer:

Get autodialler and auto-log-in device 9

Get 1200 baud modem 4

Make sure DEC is always operative 3

That one quarter of those surveyed complained about the dialling and log-in procedure in free responses illustrates that users (despite admitting the need for, and requiring, security) wish to walk to a terminal and after one or two key presses access a useful and usable part of the system.

Other suggestions included facilities they would like to see on the system, such as alterations in the software to fit the users' way of working better and elimination of the small inconsistencies and confusions. The main suggested alteration relates to the structuring of the software. At the time of the survey it was a two-level hierarchical tree structure and this was considered to be akin to an imposed filing structure. Further questioning revealed that a major difficulty was maintaining an updateable overview of the contents in relation to where one was. These were discussed in more detail in Section 2 (see also Pullinger, 1984a).

(3) User Support

User support was considered to be most satisfactory; in particular the knowledge that there was one person responsible for this, with an answerphone upon which messages could be left, was said to be most reassuring, in the sense of knowing that there was a lifebelt available should one end in the water. The other aspect of there being a 'known' human person in this role at the end of a telephone line or receiving messages on the BLEND system was that of a sounding board. With access problems and the pains of learning new software, members would occasionally want a person to whom they could express frustration etc.

Documentation was generally felt to be satisfactory, although not tested by the majority of users to its limits. Only two expressed reservations and this was to do with the appropriateness of printed documentation of that nature.

There were no additional suggestions for user support as LINC members thought the BLEND system was more than adequately supplied with this, given their level of interaction with it.

(4) Scientific Communication

It is useful to place progress in scientific communication in the context of aims expressed for their participation in the BLEND project. Figure 27 is derived from free responses to a question on the reasons for participation during the interviews around the end of 1980 before use of the BLEND system.

(Number of interviewees analysed = 21, numbers given for appreciation of proportions)

10 CONTACT
— to make new contacts and build up old contacts
15 CLOSED USER GROUP ASPECTS
— see papers before publication
— knowledge pool of ideas
— develop and record ideas (and feedback)
— closer touch with CHF (including access to previously published work)
14 PAPER PRODUCTION
— BLEND system helps users to produce or publish papers that would not otherwise have been done
— if research in CHF is enhanced
8 ELECTRONIC JOURNAL EXPERIMENTATION
— participation in experiment and what this tells us about electronic journals
8 GENERAL
— if there is some return for investment of time
— if users LIKE the BLEND system

Figure 27. Expressed Reasons for Participation of LINC Members

---

In the first six months there had been some limited progress according to expressed aims. New contacts had been made leading to exchange of ideas (mainly through other communication media) and old contacts re-affirmed although not necessarily maintained by regular communication. A certain amount of inhibition had been expressed in approaching 'strangers' of repute in interaction via an unfamiliar medium having no established protocols. No active closed user group had been formed and although the schedule for paper production was behind that anticipated, there were papers in the Poster Papers Journal, in files for editing and in the editorial procedure being refereed, besides the many reported in preparation.

From the discussion earlier concerning access problems to terminals and reasons for low use, it might be expected that certain aspects of progress in preparation of papers might fall behind members' expectations. Other reasons suggested were in the lack of any active and interactive group of users, in that many members had looked for this in a teleconferencing communication medium.

Two members surveyed pointed out that users of technology do so for a purpose: two examples might be communication or information seeking. In the first five months of use there were no purposes of this nature arising and users were basically in isolation from one another learning the system. In this respect they do not seem to have had a goal of making information, which they might have, available to others but on the other hand decidedly sought to see such information from others. Members felt inhibited in putting forward ideas to unknown people, as well as in choosing an area of discussion and in being prepared to air research ideas for which they may feel proprietary rights.

One route suggested to bypass such inhibitions was to create a very small group of regular users discussing one small aspect of Computer Human Factors, into which others may be drawn as the group interacts and extends the boundary of knowledge and creates an information and ideas pool.

This problem is experienced in any new group who might not already be interacting, and the BLEND management team had organised yearly face-to-face meetings in order for persons involved to be able to communicate more readily.

For some members it can be seen from the reasons for participation (Figure 27) that if the main expressed reason is production of papers, then when problems in the interaction with, and use of, BLEND are experienced, retreating into their main priority would mean non-use of the system but satisfaction with participation nevertheless. Non-use of the system may thus not mean non-participation for these members.

General Discussion

The results presented above seemed to indicate an emerging pattern of behaviour from which we could draw some conclusions to aid in developing the system. In particular the difficulties experienced, as expressed by LINC members, fell into clearly defined areas.

The difficulties in use of the system may be separated into five distinct operational areas: not remembering to use the system; difficult or no access to a terminal when needed; slow and unfamiliar access to the DEC computer at Birmingham; software containing small inconsistencies and in which one may get 'lost'; little return from contents for investment of time and effort.

It might therefore be reasonably hypothesised what the needs of this particular group of users are at this stage of community development. There may, however, have been other factors that might have been experienced as important if the whole system had been organised differently. For example if the level of user support had been low, then the feeling of non-support might have been manifest. Thus the following ring of five factors (Figure 28) is peculiar to the 'snapshot' of this community and is widely ranging in cost profiles for different LINC members. It illustrates that considering only certain sections of the BLEND system and improving usability at those points may not be sufficient to reduce the difficulties experienced by some users. Before the BLEND system could be successfully used, each of the five factors presented in the ring should be perceived as not presenting a costly difficulty.

In conclusion, from the six-month survey the project management team considered that progress was satisfactory and that much of value had been learnt from the LINC members' replies. The generally positive response on many areas was encouraging and confirmed a participation 'in spirit' if not always in use of the BLEND system. The learning from the phone survey has been substantial in discovering the issues in integrating such a system into a professional worklife and has many lessons for the introduction of new technology into similar situations.

5.6 Progress Following the Six-Month Survey

As a result of the six-month survey the following actions were taken by the project management team. All were aimed to improve BLEND with regard to the five factors of Figure 28.

1. Poster suggested to increase visibility. This was produced by a graphics designer and sent to each LINC member.

2. Discretionary financial help offered to those with difficult terminal access to pay for installation of external phone lines to their offices.

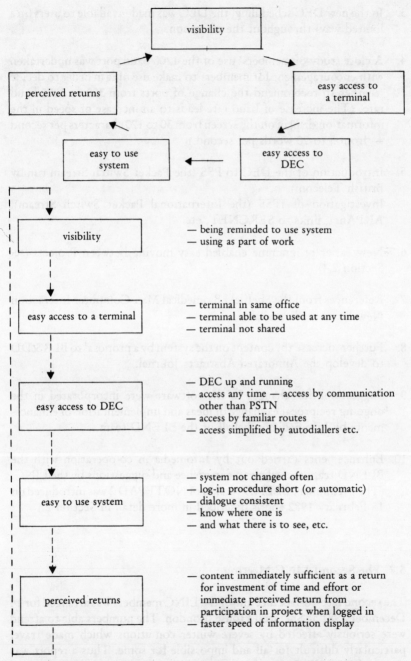

visibility

perceived returns

easy access to a terminal

easy to use system

easy access to DEC

| visibility | — being reminded to use system
— using as part of work |

| easy access to a terminal | — terminal in same office
— terminal able to be used at any time
— terminal not shared |

| easy access to DEC | — DEC up and running
— access any time — access by communication other than PSTN
— access by familiar routes
— access simplified by autodiallers etc. |

| easy to use system | — system not changed often
— log-in procedure short (or automatic)
— dialogue consistent
— know where one is
— and what there is to see, etc. |

| perceived returns | — content immediately sufficient as a return for investment of time and effort or immediate perceived return from participation in project when logged in
— faster speed of information display |

Figure 28. 'The Necessary Cycle?' — Five Factors in a Ring, which were Reported in the 1981 Survey as Necessary for Extensive Use of the BLEND System

3. In the new DEC scheduling, the DEC was made available to users (in a limited way) throughout the afternoon.

4. A close study of members' use of the 1200 baud port was undertaken with encouragement for members to make use of it in order to decide whether to recommend the change of ports from 300 to 1200 baud rate. (The increase of baud rate leads to an increase of speed in the information display on the screen from 30 to 120 characters per second — from 5 to 20 words per second.)

5. Introduction of the DEC to PSS (the Packet Switch Stream run by British Telecom).
    Investigation of IPSS (the International Packet Switch Stream), ARPAnet, links to SERCNET, etc.

6. New easier programme enabled easy moving between Projects (see Section 2.4).

7. References from the Sheffield Biomedical Man-Computer Interaction Newsletter made available.

8. Further increase the content on the system by a proposal to BLR&DD to develop the Annotated Abstracts Journal.

9. Suggestions for changes in the software were incorporated in the ongoing reciprocal exchange of ideas and implementation of enhancements by Infomedia on behalf of the BLEND team.

10. Enhancements carried out by Infomedia in co-operation with the BLEND team according to experience and suggestions by the LINC. (The preliminary BLEND version of NOTEPAD 2 was introduced on 15 February 1982 and is described in more detail in Section 2.)

5.7 The Second LINC Meeting

The second face-to-face meeting of the LINC members was arranged for 14 December 1981 at Sheraton House, London. The numbers able to attend were seriously affected by severe winter conditions which made travel particularly difficult for all and impossible for some. Thus a report was prepared (BLEND Project Management Team, 1982) to lead to a general discussion on-line in the form of open messages and a formal teleconference.

Topics covered included communication enhancements, the relationship between communication speeds and printing material off the system, the editorial procedure and the introduction of commercial/industrial researchers to be admitted to LINC.

5.8 Users' Teleconferences

The first teleconference was started on 23 August 1982 and was very popular in that all the active users participated. Figure 29 shows the activity in the teleconference over a period of 14 weeks, with the seventh

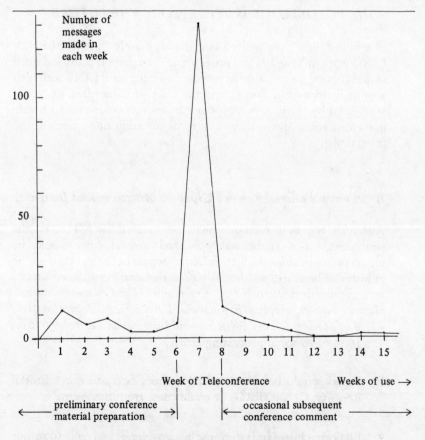

Figure 29. Frequency of Messages in Users' Teleconference 4–8 October 1982

week being named the teleconference week itself and having 136 conference entries. This teleconference was chaired by Dr. Pat Wright and covered a wide range of topics.

This led directly on to the 'Users' Conference — Ideas for BLEND-LINC Year 3' which was a teleconference preparatory to the third face-to-face LINC meeting. The teleconference was organised by Professor Brian Shackel over the period 1-18 November 1982 and a printed report was subsequently prepared (Shackel, 1982b). The conference was started by some ideas put forward by Professor Shackel based on the previous teleconference, which are now quoted in full:

SOME POSSIBLE IDEAS TO EXPLORE THE FUTURE

Five linked ideas have evolved as a possible basis for further BLEND-LINC work in Year 3 of this programme. The present plans and work would continue, especially the prepared opening up of LINC widely to anyone interested in Europe and the USA. If these ideas, or others stimulated by them, gain acceptance by enough volunteers to enable implementation, then they will form an additional part of the programme.

1. Set up an Editorial Research Group for Refereeing Real Journal(s)

Although the best method might be to establish CHF, or the equivalent, as a traditional published journal, this would be unacceptable because the British Library would be competing with the industry. Therefore, we should seek agreement from the editors of several published journals (e.g. *Ergonomics, The Computer Journal, Human Factors, Applied Ergonomics, J.A.S.I.S., J. Documentation, I.J. Man-Machine Studies, Behaviour and Information Technology*) to act as a form of editorial processing centre.

1. Papers would be submitted by authors direct to our Editorial Research Group (ERG) or could come from the journals.

2. ERG guarantees full refereeing by two referees and reply to author within 60 days of acknowledgement to author of receipt of MSS.

3. ERG guarantees refereeing of revised MSS (in response to referees' comments) within 30 days of acknowledgement of receipt.

4. Papers are sent to the journal of the author's choice with full comments of referees (identified by name and address).

5. The journal editors do not engage to accept papers but do agree to consider them favourably and rapidly. They will be expected to publish a footnote to papers such as 'this paper was refereed via the British Library BLEND-LINC experimental Editorial Research Group'.

6. The scheme will be announced by a short paper in each journal giving the details, names of members of ERG (not called 'Editorial Board' for obvious reasons), etc.

7. ERG target membership is 12 to 20. All must guarantee to referee three to four papers in the year, each within 30–45 days (first reading, and within 15–20 days for reviewing revised MSS). Papers for refereeing will be announced to all ERG members who may 'bid' for those which interest them.

8. All will have access to the advanced technology specified in 3 below.

A final short paper reviewing this experiment, naming all participants and summarising the results, will be offered to the journals involved.

2. Set Up a Future Ideas Group to try out the Forefront Technology

The aim of this group would be to explore, by proper experimental use, how authors, editors, referees, etc., may come to use the type of facilities expected to be widespread in 5–10 years.

1. Each member of the Future Ideas Group (FIG) must undertake to explore experimentally the use of the technology facilities provided.

2. All such studies must first be briefly described in a 'proposal' so that all members of FIG can offer suggestions and avoid overlap.

3. While these experimental studies should be oriented toward scientific communication (in the widest sense), there is no wish to limit the scope of ideas. A report on the study must be written for BLEND-LINC and later publication.

4. Collaborative studies and report writing between two or more members at different locations will be strongly encouraged.

5. To gain experience rapidly at the start, it is suggested that each FIG member revises a recent paper to use all the facilities available (especially colour and sound) and sends it to all FIG members.

6. All FIG members agree to participate in a final teleconference amongst themselves, leading to a definitive paper (authored jointly by several?) giving results and recommendations for how to use these facilities in future.

   It is likely that in many cases members of FIG will be at the same locations, and quite often be the same persons, as members of ERG.

3. Provide Forefront Technology at Selected Locations

To enable the ideas proposed in 1 and 2 above, so that results from the third year of the BLEND-LINC program may be adequately projective, a set of identical machines should be purchased and provided on loan to a number of appropriate locations (about 8-12). The desired facilities are as follows:—

1. auto-dial and auto-login;

2. fast communication speed via telephone system (at least 1200 baud);

3. the capability to remain switched on and 'listening' for telephone line message calls 24 hours per day for at least one year;

4. auto-receive and store messages and text sent over the telephone line;

5. signal to be displayed, until acknowledged, when message received via communication link (and can be inhibited e.g. during experiments);

6. acceptable video display screen and connection to printer;

7. enhanced facilities such as ability to display colours and synthesised or recorded sound (and also to receive Prestel and store frames?);

8. communication capability to connect to DEC20 and also directly to machines at the other research and ideas group locations.

One machine at least exists with most of the specified facilities (the TORCH microcomputer) at a price which is possible within the program.

4. *Organise an Experiment on Split-screen as an aid to Refereeing*

Very few machines exist with the capability to enable split-screen use (surprisingly one of these is the CBM PET 8032). However, this should be explored since it appears to be a desirable facility for refereeing (the ideal solution may be nearer to the 'windows' method built into the Xerox 8010 'Star' system, but this is very expensive at present).

To enable a proper experiment, one location (Birmingham?) should be provided with a suitable machine to enable development of software for split-screen working. The software must permit standard operation as a terminal to read and referee BLEND-LINC papers, and must be configured for scrolling sideways to write comments in the simplest possible way. This development must not take more than say six months. The equipment must then be movable to several other locations to enable experimental use for refereeing/editing with several (e.g. six to eight) experts to be the experimental subjects.

5. *Organise a Series of Teleconferences on Specifications for the Future*

As expected, LINC members with experience of other systems have been able to indicate limitations in BLEND (mainly a function of the NOTEPAD software). Several have expressed willingness to participate in a teleconference on mailing and conferencing systems.

This leads to the idea that several such studies could usefully be conducted to discuss and define 'user-oriented' specifications for prototype 'ideal' systems to subserve:—

1. mailing activities;

2. conferencing activities;

3. journal activities;

4. all three combined.

Of course, it may be that these discussions will suggest the above distinctions to be inappropriate and will lead to more valid concepts.

It is envisaged that the known interested and experienced members will take the lead in joining and running such teleconferences, but all LINC members will be able to participate. If this idea is supported the relevant members will be invited to chair such conferences as they agree to be appropriate.

CONCLUSION

While the above ideas are all possible, and can be developed into practical schemes, they are tentative and not intended as definitive. It is hoped they will stimulate other concepts and suggestions in response.

5.9 The Third LINC Meeting

At the third LINC face-to-face meeting held in Birmingham on 23 November 1982, members were presented with a summary of the responses and discussion as to the suggestions, and the following decisions were reached:

1. The main emphasis should be on experimental refereeing on-line and the LINC should not attempt to be attached to a publisher and create an Editorial Research Group.

2. It was accepted that there was insufficient new technology readily available to initiate the Future Ideas Group other than by the following item.

3. Members would put forward proposals for work to be done using more advanced telecommunicating terminals, the TORCHes.

4. Several looked forward to experiments on refereeing, split-screen being one option available in these.

5. Three members immediately offered to create teleconferences to discuss specific issues, including one of those mentioned, and to produce a joint paper at the end of the conference.

5.10 Purchase of the TORCH Microcomputers

In January 1983 the BLR&DD approved the purchase of 13 TORCH microcomputers for a small sub-group of volunteers, as discussed at the LINC face-to-face meeting. The TORCH offered the following facilities that were deemed worthy of their purchase:

— British designed and built

— based on the popular BBC micro

— met certain ergonomic considerations such as detachable keyboard

— allowed experimentation with colour and sound

— contained integral modem 1200/75

— permitted TORCH-TORCH communication if colour/sound could not be stored in text files on the DEC 20

— permitted automatic dialling

— permitted automatic log-in to mainframe computer

— permitted low-cost telephone use for batch delivery of files at night.

The units started to arrive at the end of January and were distributed to LINC members as appropriate. In return for the use of the TORCH to simplify access and enable new aspects of electronic publishing to be tested, members undertook to accomplish programmes of research which are described later in the fourth LINC face-to-face meeting.

5.11 The MAILBOX Teleconference

One of the invitations to start a teleconference (Section 5.8, number 5) was taken up by Mr. Paul Wilson of the National Computing Centre. He initiated the meta discussion with the following message:

[1] Wilson (Paul) 3-May-83 8:52 AM
Planning The Teleconference

. . . .

It seems to me that the first thing we must do is to plan the work of this teleconference, and that in order to do that we need to identify clear objectives. How do you feel about the following objective: 'To identify appropriate mailbox structures to meet those communication needs of scientists which are currently met by scientific journals'
Paul

This teleconference received 315 Entries (public messages) in seven months and generated a small active subgroup, which then debated, discussed and wrote a joint paper without having met each other face-to-face.

[315] Wilson (Paul) 19-Dec-83 8:56 AM
Progress with the Teleconference Paper on Active Mailboxes

. . . .

I am pleased to announce that the paper entitled 'The Active Mailbox — Your On-line Secretary' has now been completed and has been submitted to the organisers of the IFIP conference on Computer Message Services due to be held in Nottingham in May 1984. The authors of the paper were Wilson, Maude, Marshall and Heaton. Several other BLEND members were acknowledged for their contribution to the paper in this Activity.

The participant members of this exercise of joint writing plan to write a fuller description of the process in a subsequent paper.

5.12 The Software Reviews Journal

Dr. Thomas Green of the Social and Applied Psychology Unit, University of Sheffield, offered to start a new journal entitled *Software Reviews*. He gave the aims in his first editorial:

[1] Green (Thomas) 12-Jul-83 9:34 PM

EDITORIAL

1 AIMS

An interactive journal of software reviews. First off, who's listening? I'm going to aim primarily at the immediate needs of scientific writers who are not computing specialists. That means giving major weight to preparing documents, especially papers — we need to be able to structure a paper, handle different formats for the main text, the tables, and the bibliography, and possibly number the sections and insert footnotes. Spelling checkers, grammar checkers, and text formatters are important; so are simple statistics packages and aids to preparing graphs for graphics printers or plotters. There may be a small number of book reviews, too.

I assume that the target community's machines are mainly CP/M machines, Apples, and Beebs. Less weight will be given to software for other machines, or to reviewing implementations of programming languages, spread-sheet calculators, utilities programs, and databases; and virtually none to financial programs, integrated office environments, or (shh!) games. Unless it turns out that there's a demand, of course. Occasional accounts of state-of-the-art systems for document-processing will be warmly welcome.

2 STRUCTURE

The journal will include review articles, a comments section for each review, and a column for Letters to the Editor. Reviews will be organised by area: text, graphics, languages, statistics and other numerical tasks, database handling, and utilities. When integrated systems crop up I'll make *ad hoc* decisions.

95

Everyone is welcome to submit. First, REVIEWS: do please review any interesting software you can get at. Don't worry if someone else is already reviewing 'your' software: the beauty of this system is that we have no page restrictions. I shall try to arrange for reviews of the same software to be cross-referenced or even adjacent.

The progress of the journal is described later in the report of the fourth LINC face-to-face meeting.

5.13 The *References, Abstracts and Annotations Journal*

One of the other results in the six-month survey was to include on the BLEND system more references to published material. An application to BLR&DD led to the initiation of the *References, Abstracts and Annotations Journal,* started in May 1983. This is fully described in Section 3.2.

5.14 35-Month Phone Survey

In the $2\frac{1}{2}$ years following the six-month survey, two major versions of the software had been introduced and the experimental programme extended to September 1984. As part of this extended programme, 10 LINC members have been provided with TORCH microcomputers to facilitate access to BLEND and upon which to undertake related experimental work to be reported on the BLEND system.

Viewing the wider context, the importance of Human Factors had been recognised in that one of the special advisory groups for national development set up as a result of the Alvey Report is on Man-Machine Interaction. Computer Human Factors, the subject area of the LINC, has also been viewed as having much to contribute to industry following the British government's push to advertise information technology in 1982.

Within this background, the project team members at Loughborough University of Technology instigated a repeat phone survey of the LINC with similar aims and questions to the six-month survey in June–July 1981.

Discussion on Phone Survey

Attempts were made during the week of 14–18 November 1983 to contact each member of the LINC. Excepted were all the new members who had responded to recent invitations and the few senior members who had been invited to join for initial observation.

One hundred and one calls were made, six of which reached the person required at the first attempt and 32 of which were successful in the end. At the time of the survey there were 92 scientific members (including the research team), of whom 26 had recently joined. Of the remaining 66, 30 had been interviewed in the six-month survey and 22 of these were successfully reached for the survey reported here. Many of the others had not logged on other than for demonstration or trial purposes.

General Response

The general response to being called by phone was very positive and all members seemed prepared to give up time answering questions and expressing their views openly.

In particular there was a generally pervading opinion that the research undertaken on and with BLEND was worthwhile and needed increasing. The views were subject to the assumption that many opinions were already put on the system and so were not necessarily worth repeating in the interview. Thus, this survey, like the six-month survey, should be taken as a 'snapshot' of the attitudes of the LINC members interviewed.

Members considered all aspects of the system and many suggestions were forthcoming, although different solutions were often offered for the same unexpressed underlying problem. Thus the numbers making specific suggestions appear low but the proportion of those wishing to concur with similar comments might be considered an indicator of the analytical or attitudinal response to that particular area.

An analysis of the area in which members spent most time talking (as noted during or immediately after the interview) revealed that two aspects, access (13 people) and the BLEND software (10 people), still cause the most difficulty or initiated some other subjective response. A small group (four people) was concerned about making the on-line members more communicative and creating an active community.

Discussion of Results

1. Use of the BLEND system

LINC members were asked how much they used the BLEND system. Of those interviewed, over two-thirds were up-to-date with proceedings, having regularly logged in once a month or more frequently (see Figure 30).

Average	0 (recently)	4	Number of LINC
frequency	A few times	10	members in each
of use of	Once per month	3	frequency
BLEND by	Once per week	2	category
LINC members	2 or 3 times per week	7	
interviewed	3 or 4 times per week	6	
		32	

Figure 30. Frequency of Use for LINC Members Interviewed

This accords well with the use of the system as recorded in NOTEPAD. Of those that logged in, over three-quarters were up-to-date in the Messages activity. However, only 4 in 10 of all LINC members had logged into this area and only half had logged in since the second major change of software in May 1983, the others dipping into different journals.

Several commented on the use of TORCH microcomputers as changing their patterns of use from occasional long sessions to short daily sessions whenever they were in the office. Those in the frequency category 'two to three times a week' were split into regular and irregular users, the former accessing BLEND daily when opportunity was given and the latter having spells of high activity followed by weeks of being away completely, owing to other engagements and external pressures.

Reference has already been made to some of the types of external pressures and these were cited as the main reasons for disuse by those who had only logged in a few times. Those who had not logged in at all were in the position of having moved jobs or types of job (two people) or not having had time to organise things (two people).

A total of 23 people thought that they had all the equipment that they needed. The nine remaining had varied requirements ranging from the lack of a printer to go with a TORCH or microcomputer to total lack of equipment situated where they could use it. Only three people surveyed could not log in satisfactorily. The members exhibiting an above average use tended to have more equipment and more ways in which to access the BLEND system. Figure 31 illustrates the variety of ways in which users could choose alternatives.

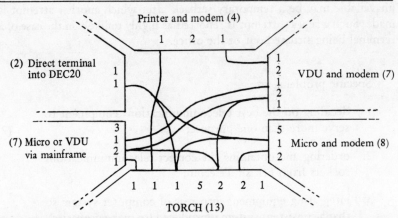

The lines indicate choice of equipment. For example, starting in any box, if that particular piece of equipment is not operational, then following the lines will indicate the other possibilities. The number below it gives the number of members with that combination. The members with larger choice tend to use the system more.

Figure 31. Variety of Alternative Equipment for 29 Members

Access for 13 members had been dramatically altered by the availability of the TORCH microcomputers. Moreover, 23 were entirely satisfied with their access, whether this was because the terminal equipment was in their own office, at home, conveniently situated in a nearby office or distant from the office. It is to be noted that when the terminal equipment was sited at hand in an office or at home, general remarks were made to the effect that use patterns altered from occasional sessions consisting of several hours to short sessions two or three times a week. However, some users prefer the longer session away from the office where one is uninterrupted by phone calls and visits.

Nine users have terminals distant from them or in a room close by which is found inconvenient for some reason. This is most often reported as being due to the terminal equipment being in a particular person's office and people's disinclination to move away from their own office to another however strong the invitation. Many of these expressed the benefits of a terminal in the office as (a) creating a visible reminder to use the system, (b) removing the effort barrier of access and (c) enabling one to fill in two or three minutes before coffee (or similar) period by logging in. In particular there are differences in behavioural patterns resulting from an unsuccessful attempt to use the system. When a terminal is in your room, then failure to connect due to busy telephone lines or the BLEND system being unavailable may be a temporary setback after which another attempt is made. Such a repeat attempt is reported as highly unlikely in the case of a terminal being situated out of the office.

Specific problems are:

1. deciding on the best telecommunications equipment to serve more than one purpose; (2)

2. ordering and obtaining the correct telecommunications sockets from British Telecom; (2)

3. integrating equipment into rest of computer system so that a consistent system is produced (to make use easier). This is applicable to equipment, terminal software and telecommunication routes such as PSTN, PSS and SERCNET; (2)

4. flexibility of equipment in both what is used (e.g. printer or VDU) and where it is positioned; (1)

5. having access to BLEND system between 9 a.m. and 5 p.m. (considered 'absolutely essential'); (4)

6. communication between NOTEPAD and other message systems such as ARPAnet and COM. (1)

2. Changes to Software

No direct satisfaction rating was sought on the software and the only question in this survey related to proposed changes. Nevertheless there were many positive comments with three members saying that the software was quite easy to use and that they were quite happy with it. Two others noted the vast improvement over the past three years and that this observation appeared to be genuine and could not be attributed entirely to getting used to the 'nasties'.

Project Activity Structure and Message-handling

There were six comments relating to the fact that the NOTEPAD teleconferencing suite was not designed for the job of electronic journals and hence was proving 'generally cumbersome' and requiring, as a result, a change of level of interaction. The level of interaction being too restricted was most strongly noted in the Project structure necessitating a separate log-in of name, password and terminal-type (10 people), and in being aware of new information, which at present necessitates entering into a Project to find out whether there are any new messages (nine people). This Project compartmentalisation means that people report getting confused because they are not sure what is where (four people).

There seemed to be two areas of suggestions to deal with this problem, the first to have more VDU-oriented software (three people) and supply a presentation control system (one person) and the second to develop the information and message-handling in general:—

Message Retrieval and Handling Suggestions

Know when there is new information in different Projects and Activities.	9
Get all private messages (Notes) in an underlying mail system.	2
Have facility to flag a message or mark as 'skimmed but not digested'.	4
Have facility to throw all messages away and say 'Tough, you missed them'.	1
Have facility to block all messages to be free to do other work.	1
Have better facilities for search and retrieval of messages.	2
Have better facilities for knowing content of messages before seeing them.	1
Have better facilities for grouping and combining messages.	2

Editing and Reading Messages

Writing and reading messages also provoked suggestions for improvement with emphasis on improving the editing facilities (six people), specifically having screen editing (four people), and having faster speed of communication (five people) with perhaps a variable control on scrolling rate (one person). The necessity to have programs especially for reading and browsing (READ, BROWSE) meant that these are not fully integrated into the BLEND system (one person). The lack of graphics facilities was keenly felt by three members. The specific suggestions for editing and reading were:—

Editing and Reading Information

Better interaction with editing facilities.	1
Introduce screen editing.	4
Introduce an intermediate editor (less complex than EDIT & EM).	2
Multiple comment facility on sections of text.	1
Faster access in telecommunication speed.	5
Variable scroll speed.	1
Variable line spacing.	1
Uniform way of reading text.	1
Software to get only summaries of papers.	1
How to stop reading messages and skip to next one.	2
Have better low-level graphics.	3

Other Suggestions

There remains with some users (two people) a terminology confusion between certain pairs of words: Action and Activity; Activity and Project. Further the soft numbering of the menu choice of the Activities in each Project leads to confusion because when a user refers to an Activity by menu choice number it may be different for other users (one person).

The other suggestions related to other parts of the software: removal of the log-in to the DEC (in contrast to the BLEND software) (one person); the ability to change what terminal-type the computer thinks that the user has in the middle of the interaction (one person), for example, for printing several messages or a paper; improving the facilities for changing the *role* of user to make them more flexible (one person).

3. The Content of the BLEND System and the Use of the Software

There were many views on the sort of journal wanted and type of use to which a communication system like BLEND might be put. Many look forward to a greater development of communication levels that cannot be easily accomplished by other more traditional media of communication, and the question was raised as to whether enough exploration was being done with different levels.

Over a quarter of those responding thought the quality of the content was good (one noting the Human Factors bias in general) and a half thought it variable. The variability is not necessarily a criticism, as one member noted, it is to be expected in just the same way as programmes are variable on T.V. channels. The quantity was considered good by one person but over three-quarters thought that more was needed, especially in the *Computer Human Factors* journal. The reasons put forward for a higher quantity were that more material would lead to more interaction and that the change in cost-benefit ratio would begin to make logging-in more worthwhile.

The lack of interaction concerned five members who put forward suggestions to invite more members to join and to create situations, as in teleconferences, in which the user is forced to respond. The lack of interaction from a number of people also had the deleterious effect of seeming to create a clique of those who contributed (comment by two people). Partly this was explained by the emergence of those who had both easy to use equipment readily accessible and who had managed to integrate it more into their working patterns and partly also because of the lack of urgency in the type of material. The Leicester Polytechnic Research Group had, for example, become network based quite rapidly and would be 'lost' without this type of facility. The reason for the success of the interaction was suggested to be the helpfulness of people in responding to urgent pleas for help of the kind 'My PERQ has gone wrong in the following way, can anyone help?' This kind of interaction can be seen in the TORCH Users Group Conference on BLEND. It was suggested further that the lack of interaction might partly be caused by not achieving the correct level of communications and hence there was need to do more exploration at different levels and exploitation of the electronic medium (three people).

The members liked the more newsy aspects of the information, with specific mention of News and *LINC News* (five people), *Software Reviews* (two people), Bulletins (two people), the concept of the *References, Abstracts and Annotations Journal* (six people). These last six also commented that it does not yet turn out to be informative; perhaps (as one member proposed) one needs a very large number of people commenting. Although two people liked the Poster Papers, both thought that other text could be shorter and lighter, a point made more forcibly by seven members who suggested that Poster Papers should not be in CHF journal form at all but be short papers designed to elicit discussion and debate. One suggestion was to have a 'paper of the month' in this form — whether the paper was on or off the BLEND system initially. Another member disliked the separation of paper and discussion in the CHF journal.

General messages were accepted as useful (if News) but it was noted that it was often unclear for whom they were written and so they seemed to reduce to a personal expression or statement (one person). Some are evidently ephemeral (two people) and these make it harder to find information embedded in the serial accumulation of messages (two people). For this reason, more specific guidance on the whereabouts of types of information was sought (two people). Even when the flow of discussion was uninterrupted by ephemeral messages, members said they experienced difficulty in entering a discussion already started and spoke of being 'overwhelmed' by the number of messages (two people). Despite these difficulties, the reader will see that the majority of the discussion and suggestions in this section relate to increasing the interaction between BLEND users by a variety of ways and indeed six people specifically suggested having more discussion groups. The teleconference in 1982 led by Professor Brian Shackel and the Mailbox Teleconference led by Mr. Paul Wilson were both given as illustrations of good examples, although there needs to be more incentive for prospective leaders, perhaps by having well-set hard-copy output or another such goal (one person).

4. User Support

There was much appreciation for the development of the Users' Guides and Manuals over the 2½ years. All members expressed general satisfaction with the form, style and usefulness of them, except for five users for whom the question was not applicable. All were satisfied with the wider user support for the BLEND system, which comprises a member's card, on-line help and query service, and a telephone answering service. The last was specifically mentioned by one-third as being a 'lifebelt'. In general, the feeling was summed up by the comment 'When I need support it's there'.

There were, however, some suggestions for further improvements to assist users. More on-line aid was thought useful, e.g. a comprehensive recall facility for all commands and a synopsis of what was going on in the system. However, the majority of the 15 suggestions concerned the need for more technical assistance in connecting up equipment and in communications. Of the 13 TORCH users six complained bitterly about the standard of TORCH communication and felt that more assistance in the area of both software and hardware was desirable.

5. Scientific Communication

The largest category of reported scientific communication with others was 'casual'. However, some respondents commented very favourably on the opportunities that being LINC members had presented, e.g. enabling them to get to know names of experts in the Computer Human Factors field and creating a sense of 'community' (four people). The most common way in which this operated was to meet people at seminars, meetings or conferences and to be recognised as another LINC member (three people). For some, research had been initiated by participation which would not otherwise have been encountered (two people) and others considered research being undertaken (in the Mailbox Teleconference on the BLEND system) as worthwhile and 'hard work'.

Paper production and preparation generally divided the members into active and non-active groups in that a greater proportion of those who had

None	8
Casual	15
Medium	4
Hard work	2
N/A	3
	32

Figure 32. Reported Scientific Communication through BLEND Project Participation

produced several papers for BLEND also had one or more pieces of writing in preparation. Fifty per cent of those interviewed reported papers in preparation.

There are many levels of communication on BLEND in semi-formal and formal pieces of text, ranging from Poster Papers and *Software Reviews* to papers for the Refereed Papers Journal, CHF. All of these have been considered in the table above.

Papers produced	N/A	0	1	2	3+
Number of members	3	10	9	5	5
Number with papers in preparation			4	3	4	4

Figure 33. Papers Produced and in Preparation

6. General Points

Members noted the experimental nature of the BLEND project (four people) and also its uniqueness. The concept of an electronic journal is a fascinating one and it is satisfying to be at the leading edge of information technology (two people) and part of the excitement. In terms of directness and speed of access the idea remains very attractive at a conceptual level (two people) but in practice a number of problems remain (one person). The BLEND team was urged to persevere with the idea (one person). In view of this perceived experimental nature it is worth exploring and using all the options available (one person), but also taking serious account of facilities not yet available, such as graphics, since the difference that small changes might make to acceptability at a future point may be significant (one person).

The interviewer had the impression that others viewed the BLEND system more as a service and the need for good access to equipment, good telecommunications and access to the DEC20 was emphasised in the context of what the research findings may reveal. (Access was discussed earlier in this section.)

It was pointed out that perhaps the climate is not yet right for the use of electronic journals (two people), that putting papers on-line is not terribly worthwhile (three people), and also that we really need to concentrate on teleconferences. The background for this seems to be that one saw the content as being more ephemeral (one person) than that which is found in academic journals, that such a system should be treated like a newspaper (one person) or a mailbox (two people) with additional facilities such as teleconferencing and bulletin boards (two people). Specifically these two members suggested systems like the Berkeley UNIX mail and front-end combined with COM teleconferencing and having papers stored on bulletin boards.

The interest in the appropriateness of NOTEPAD and BLEND led to a request to be brought up-to-date with the Human Factors work on networking (one person). One of the factors raised was the 'compulsive' response in having to talk to people if one met them on the system — thereby distracting one from a task of work (one person). Two enjoyed being members and suggested that this had stimulated their research.

General Discussion

There can be no doubt that the majority of the LINC members interviewed are in a sense 'the survivors' and hence more likely to have sorted out access problems one way or another. It is perhaps worth noting again that 23 out of 32 were entirely happy with their equipment, which is reflected in the areas of interest expressed by the members being more concerned with the changes needed in the software rather than only the problems of access.

Changes in the software have also been considerable and this is shown in increased use and also in users having given a greater consideration to the more underlying design features of the BLEND system and NOTEPAD.

The next three sections make short observations on this latter area, the design of a BLEND-type system, the ways to increase interaction and user support for the TORCH microcomputer, respectively.

Content – 'We want more – we want less'

There were many LINC members who commented on the 'overwhelming' number of messages and new information that appeared on the BLEND system, particularly if they had not had the opportunity to log in for a week or two. At the same time (and sometimes by the same people) there was an expression of there not being enough material on the system. It seems that we have here the focal point of the difficulties with designing a system which allows all levels of communication from short messages to papers. Expressed in another way, we have the problems associated with designing an integrated store of messages and information which is considerably more archival in nature than only an electronic mail system but 'active' compared to an archived database for information retrieval. One solution is to simplify the problem by separation of the two parts and this seems to be the reason why two members said that they would prefer a full mail system or a teleconference system with a bulletin board for papers.

First, let us consider the way in which the problem of being 'overwhelmed' is dealt with for messages (whether private notes or public entries). There are three general approaches: (a) compartmentalisation, (b) grouping of messages by participants and (c) individual handling in private store.

(a) NOTEPAD attempts to deal with the problem by a separation of the store of messages into discrete stores called Activities. There are two resulting difficulties which have been observed in the BLEND system. First, the structure will always be someone else's filing system (whether the 'someone else' is an individual leader or group consensus) and this poses a difficulty to the user in knowing what message should be placed in which compartment. Secondly, the compartmentalisation is difficult to maintain meaningfully since teleconferences frequently take a turn which would have made it preferable (with hindsight) to have started the discussion elsewhere or to include relevant messages from another compartment.

(b) A single database of messages which are loosely grouped by the originators of the messages to create a series of 'topics' within the general sequence. This permits the participants to control the structure and to allow messages to be part of several topics where there is relevance.

(c) A database of messages which is viewed and handled solely from a single participant's window and whose handling affects no-one else. This is the general electronic mail model existent at present whereby each sender and receiver of messages chooses individually how to store the messages.

Whichever of these three models is adopted (and this is not the place to discuss their relative merits), there were a number of suggestions by LINC members for reducing the 'overwhelming' quantity of messages, many of which have limited life and/or specific purposes. Some of these suggestions are aggregated and listed below:

(a) Have ephemeral messages with a marked life for automatic deletion. Examples include: 'The system is going down for maintenance this Friday'.

(b) Eliminate serial numbered slots for origination of messages (to the users) so that users do not have to perceive deleted messages.

(c) Because authors of messages are often responding to specific points raised by others, but find it cumbersome to make a full reference either to the Conference Entry or to the point, software such as the EIES 'TOPICS' could be developed. This would allow messages to be 'tied' to a previous one and a sequence of relevant messages followed by the reader.

(d) Facilities for skimming, scanning and flagging would reduce the necessity to look at all the messages and the need to act upon receipt or remember which messages needed to be dealt with.

(e) Optional entry into a list of messages (TOPIC) so that the time available to the user can be mapped against priority of interests.

(f) Have an optional backdated point of entry (e.g. one week) so that not all messages are displayed.

It will be noted that the three general approaches above place quite different demands on the participant and that the suggestions above all refer to a reduction of the cost in the task of receiving information. Since all three general models work reasonably well for different applications of messaging, it seems that a careful appraisal is needed of the tasks involved in the future integrated communications of a LINC-type community.

Whilst an improvement of the messaging system is clearly possible (and necessary for a BLEND type system), it is less clear how to integrate the 'archived' or 'semi-archived' material. Already BLEND users expect a notification of *all* new material throughout the system, whatever form it takes.

However, it seems that archived material is seen in different ways by different participants in terms of information flow. For some a paper might be a very large message refereed by peers and stored in exactly the same way as a message, but the problem comes again in overwhelming a particular line of messages (TOPIC) by inclusion of a large piece of text — however it is handled. It is to be noted also that some people start from messages and build into teleconferences, whereas others start from journal papers and go into messages to make comments.

Suggestions indicate that a top level of commands and interaction with choices between approaches is to be preferred, so that a discussion on a paper might be reached easily via the paper or via messages, and that both may be reached via a sophisticated information retrieval system.

Interaction – 'Why isn't there more?'

Areas of concern for some members include the lack of interactive dialogue, comment on papers and general participation. There are contributory factors already mentioned in the results above including:

— the lack of intelligent telecommunication terminals;

— poor and low-speed telecommunications;

— inadequate daytime access to the DEC20 at Birmingham;

— lack of integration between office equipment and terminals;

— small amount of time available due to external circumstances;

— small number of 'leaders' proportional to members;

— low perceived benefit for learning to operate system.

Perhaps the most surprising aspect of telecommunications is that in the three years of the BLEND programme, there has been little advance in ordinary user telecommunication terminals except for the TORCH. This remains a major problem.

As people get used to the facilities offered, they require integration of office equipment and terminals, for example in the use of word-processors or computer-filing systems. In the face of competition for written output in the subject area, several suggestions were made relating to a change in length and style of the Poster Papers and to generating more tele-conferences and types of communication that exploit the electronic medium. These may well lead to full-length academic papers later. Indeed, one suggestion included the possibility of the production of a book based on teleconferences in BLEND under the guiding leadership of different experts. This type of suggestion attempts to pull together the good aspects of electronic communication and bridge the difficulties. Hence there is participation of members who are too short of time to write a full paper, access time does not have to be great, there is integration of conceptual tasks and also some motivation in the form of deadlines and observable output.

With this is a desire to use the BLEND system when needed at all times in the day. Thus it is to be expected that the start of integration will lead to a change from viewing the BLEND system as an 'experiment' to viewing it as a 'service'. At this point, higher standards of infrastructure are expected in telecommunications, access and system and user support. On the other hand, the maintenance of an 'experimental' view leads to a separation of function in working life and little attempt at integration of normal tasks. We may note here that there is (as in many such situations) a resolution of these positions for a few researchers whose general working patterns are themselves considered conceptually as experimental.

Reference has already been made to Alvey and the raising of industrial awareness of Computer Human Factors. This interest and the increasing number of conferences have led to a shortage of current research reports and papers. Thus some persuasion is needed for researchers to produce papers. The BLEND system has felt this shift and has not so far had the requisite number of 'leaders' to motivate production of reports, etc.

TORCH User Support

Three-quarters of the TORCH owners complained about the extremely poor quality (and quantity) of the documentation and requested more user support in the use of these microcomputers. In discussion with the Project Director, it became clear that the BLEND project management team had behaved 'like typical systems designers'. They were aware both of the inadequacy of the documentation and of the BLEND team's inadequate resources to meet all the help that would be required. Thus the choice was to accept that the TORCH system was undersupported and not to use it or to take the view that it would be better than nothing. The latter view had been adopted, with the resulting satisfaction of being able to log in easily and the resulting frustration when unable to discover how to use the TORCH in an integrated way.

5.15 The Fourth LINC Meeting

The fourth LINC face-to-face meeting was arranged in the BLR&DD (office: London W1) on 20 December 1983, attended by 37 LINC members. The usual pattern was adopted consisting of reports from Loughborough and Birmingham, followed by discussion on what had happened over the previous year. Additionally, in the morning session those who had TORCHes also described their research and use of them for the BLEND programme. These descriptions follow. In the afternoon, plans, ideas and suggestions were put forward and there followed a lively debate after which decisions were made about what to change and what to keep. The discussion included: post September 1984 plans; provision of up-to-date list of LINC members on BLEND; the necessity of joint work in reviewing the usefulness of NOTEPAD software for BLEND; encouraging different styles of paper to be placed into Poster Papers; access to the experimental Prestel pages supplied by the British Library; contributions to *LINC News* from members themselves rather than the editor; future teleconferences; provision of a calendar of events to be placed on BLEND and the necessity for a trial of using BLEND with advanced technological equipment and facilities.

The descriptions of the work by the LINC members using TORCHes follow:

Software Reviews – Thomas Green

Dr. Thomas Green of Sheffield University presented a brief description of his studies with the TORCH using BLEND. He decided that there was a large demand for software, but that the current reviews of software were inadequate. Therefore, it was suggested that BLEND should be used to gather together software reviews.

A project was set up for this purpose in July/August 1983 and since then about 16 people have logged into it. The project was divided into areas which were thought to be relevant to working scientists who would use their computers as tools. The following areas were established: text processing; utilities and packages; database work, languages; numerical problems; and graphics. People were then encouraged to submit reviews.

The breakdown of articles which have appeared is: six on text processing, two on utilities, one concerning databases, one on comparison of BASIC languages, and none on numerical problems and graphics. The lengths and styles of the reviews were varied but no comment was made by readers. Similarly readers were encouraged to add remarks concerned with reviews seen in other places and to make suggestions. However, very few comments have been made. The only queries have been concerned with portable micros.

Graphics – Peter Innocent

Dr. Peter Innocent, Leicester Polytechnic, was using his TORCH to look at the feasibility of reformatting non-graphics-type information to graphics information, looking at the transformation from information in a paper to another alternative form of presentation. Thus he was concerned with taking non-textual information and producing it in a graphic form. Secondly, the requirements of readers and writers in this context were studied.

The strategy was to try to use the TORCH in some application which required graphics initially. A simulation program was used, which simulated some physiological processes using a basic Acornsoft graphics package. Although this package is cheap and widely available, there are problems in that it is slow, there is no interface to BLEND, it fills memory very quickly and there is very poor user control on the graphics. Therefore, it seems a CP/M graphics interface is needed, a standard graphics interface and the ability to tailor BLEND into such a graphics facility.

This led him to suggest the need for research into standardisation and, in particular, into open systems interconnection, which is necessary to enable BLEND to communicate across networks. There are three areas of technology which could enable such graphics and open systems inter-connection to be provided for BLEND-type systems:

(1) Low-cost graphics add-on, e.g. 'PLUTO' boards.

(2) High-quality graphics, e.g. ARGS.

(3) Flexible Workstation, e.g. PERQ.

However, the main problem is still a gap in the software.

113

Refereeing On-line – John Long and Paul Buckley

Dr. John Long from University College London explained that his TORCH had been used to get an insight into the refereeing tasks which are to be performed on-line. Paul Buckley then described the study he had conducted as part of his M.Sc. project (Buckley, 1983). The study started by analysing the refereeing task in order to try to identify what facilities would be required. In analysing the task there seemed to be two distinct stages, the first being the reading of the article and the second the construction of the critique. It was discovered that referees tended to mark positions of interesting points with non-specific marks. On the TORCH the format and search facilities were varied in the experimental design. Subjects were required to search for quotations in the text either by stepping through or by being able to jump around the text. However, these variables had very little effect on the time taken to find the required quotations.

It seems, in the future, that it would be useful to compare two approaches, single-page access or variable-rate access with a variable-grain access where the referee can go through every nth page. It seems that a facility enabling the referee to move freely and rapidly around the paper would be the most useful addition.

It was suggested that perhaps windowing on a two-dimensional plane rather than simply relying on a linear read through may be more successful. This is obviously an area for future research.

BBC Use – Chris Reynolds

Dr. Chris Reynolds has been using his TORCH in two areas of activities, mainly as a general purpose computer, using its word-processing function. However, work is also being carried out on a comparison between micro BASIC and BBC BASIC and also on a schools package for the BBC microcomputer, which involves the use of colour as a computer aid.

There are, of course, problems transferring BBC programs on to a TORCH, because of the differences in the keyboards. For example, the function keys such as the control function key vary across these keyboards. Having experienced this, Chris Reynolds offered advice to anyone who came across similar problems in the future.

Refereeing On-line – Pat Wright

Dr. Pat Wright, MRC Applied Psychology Unit, has also been conducting an experiment on refereeing. It was felt that one of the major considerations should be to provide annotation facilities for referees. However, if authors submit their editorial comments to the editor on the same screen as the author's text, there is very little space for such comments. To overcome this problem a second micro was coupled to the TORCH. Software was designed to allow annotations to be written, and its effectiveness was evaluated. Individuals were given a proof-reading task and results showed that not only were people affected by working with a screen display, but that actually the fast readers were hampered considerably more than the slow readers; it was not simply an equal legibility decrement across the board. This study has been written up for BLEND and BIT (Wright & Lickorish, 1983).

A study then followed using eight experienced referees to referee journal papers both on screen and in hard copy. Data were collected throughout. At the end of the study one of the major concerns in the on-screen condition was moving around the text in sections because subjects only had a single-page backwards and forwards movement available to them.

One major consideration for future research would be the critical issue of window size, particularly if trying to avoid overcrowding on one micro rather than two coupled together.

Mailbox Teleconference – Paul Wilson

After a brief overview of the teleconference organised by Mr. Paul Wilson of the National Computing Centre, he gave an outline of what he considered to be the future of teleconferencing. He considered image, voice and text electronic mail and mailbox systems and, realising that there was much confusion about electronic mail systems, tried to find applications for such systems.

Paul Wilson also described his study of 'structures' because it appears that structures are the underlying factors which enable mailbox systems to be useful. In a face-to-face meeting there is a typical format and thus an individual has an internal knowledge of how to conduct oneself at such a meeting, and these 'structures' enable the communication process to be useful; without these structures the communication is chaotic. Thus structures are a way of imposing order on this kind of communication to

115

enable a job to be completed and, therefore, these structures must be available in BLEND for effective communication to take place.

The structures identified can be placed into three categories:

(1) structures to organise the information generated, e.g. classification, format, storage and retrieval of messages and analysis or presentation of messages;

(2) structures for getting things done, e.g. controlling the process, allocating roles, generating material, making decisions;

(3) structures for controlling who does what, e.g. controlling communication flows, and creating communities.

The next task was to decide which structures were appropriate for which applications. This turned out to be a complex task, possibly because the structures in use already had not been identified, or the structures identified were not applicable, or there was a gap in our knowledge of structures. It is obviously of vital importance to realise and understand exactly which structures are necessary to enable a project team or working party to communicate effectively in order to produce the finished output.

There are three major problems in trying to produce a set of structures necessary for a teleconference. First, every individual works in a different way and individuals may not readily accept structures which have been offloaded on to them. Secondly, the structures themselves must be easy to use and ergonomic, and, thirdly, the structures themselves must be modifiable because for an individual task people may want to alter them slightly.

Summary of Discussion at Fourth LINC Meeting

Following the presentations, the discussion led to the following decisions:

1. The LINC should continue to think of the BLEND system and experimental programme as a design study for a future system. To this end, data should be reliably recorded by all members of the project team and members of the community in order to establish the efficacy of the facilities available in the software suite. Perhaps an on-line teleconference or joint paper may be considered to discuss the problems of using NOTEPAD.

2. The Poster Papers Journal will accept papers of any length and structure and authors are to be encouraged to place short reviews or lengthy articles there for others to read.

3. A teleconference is to be held on the subject of 'The Social Impact of Microcomputers on Adolescents', provided there is sufficient interest.

4. A calendar of conferences and other events is to be placed on the system for LINC members.

5. With many new members joining, the BLEND management team reassured the community that 'Who's Who', describing the addresses and interests of members, will be kept up-to-date.

6. One person (on or off the BLEND system) should be invited each month to present a personal view, abstract or paper for discussion by the community.

7. The LINC is to continue studying in several directions, by experience and experiment, the problems associated with refereeing on-line.

8. The LINC requested access to Prestel for a proposed experiment placing an article on to a viewdata-type system.

9. A forum was suggested in which to exchange news on BBC micro software, to be organised by a LINC member.

5.16 The Present State of the LINC

There are at present 97 members of the LINC, many joining as a result of receiving letters of invitation at the end of 1983. These were sent out with an introduction and BLEND system bibliography to known researchers of human factors of computer systems. The present members are listed in Appendix 8.

There are 11 Projects to which they have access:

NEWS   — messages, *LINC Newsletter*, etc.

PROGRESS   — discussion about organisation of BLEND system

AUTHOR	— area in which to write and/or edit papers
BULLETIN	— BLEND team papers
POSTER	— Poster Papers are submitted without refereeing
STACK-POSTER	— The long-term archive of Poster Papers
CHF1	— The first issue of Refereed Papers Journal *Computer Human Factors*
CHF2	— The second issue of Refereed Papers Journal *Computer Human Factors*
RAAJ	— The *References, Abstracts and Annotations Journal*
CC1–2	— *Computer Compacts*, Volume 1, No. 2 (articles only)
SR	— *Software Reviews.*

These are itemised more fully with details of all the present open Activities in Appendix 4.

Over 40 papers have been submitted to the journals; at least some of them are reported as not having been written otherwise.

The actual papers that have been archived in electronic form in the journals are listed under authorship in Appendices 5 and 6 for refereed and unrefereed papers respectively.

6 GLOSSARY

TERM	EXPLANATION OF TERM
Action	In the BLEND system, inside all Activities there are nine principal operations that can be commanded by the user; these *Actions* have been mapped on to the digits 1 to 9 for ease of use and are available following the prompt 'ACTION'.
Activity	An Activity is a meeting area in the BLEND system with named participants.
ARGS	A hardware package for graphics marketed by Sigma Co.
ARPAnet	Advanced Research Projects Agency Network, US Department of Defense. Now used as an experimental message service by scientists all over the world.
ASCII	American Standard Code for Information Interchange, a seven-bit binary code representing numbers, upper and lower case letters, punctuation marks and other symbols.
BASIC	One of a number of languages available for use on computers (often microcomputers).
Baud	Data transfer rate, approximately equivalent to bits per second.
Bit	The smallest unit of information, either 0 or 1 (binary digit).
BLEND	Birmingham and Loughborough Electronic Network Development. BLEND is also the name of the computer software system mounted on the Birmingham University DEC20 based on NOTEPAD software (see below).

BLR&DD	British Library Research & Development Department, 2 Sheraton Street, London W1V 4BH.
BT	British Telecom — the organisation which operates the telephone system in Britain.
BU	University of Birmingham and particularly Centre for Computing and Computer Studies.
Byte	A set of eight binary digits considered as a unit.
Character	A numeric, letter, punctuation mark or special symbol.
CHF	Computer Human Factors — a multi-disciplined area of interest for those concerned with the human/computer relationship at a variety of levels.
COM	A computer conferencing software suite developed from FORUM by Jacob Palme at the Stockholm University Computing Centre.
Computer Conferencing System	A system which uses the computer to structure, store and process written communications among a group of persons. Examples include EIES, FORUM, NOTEPAD, COM.
CP/M	Operating system for microcomputer, developed by Garry Kildall of Digital Research in the USA.
CPU	Central Processing Unit — the principal operating part of a computer.
Data	Information to be input to, or output from, a system.
DEC20	The host computer for the BLEND system located at the University of Birmingham.
Display	Visual representation of data, e.g. VDU.

EIES	Electronic Information Exchange System — system operating in the USA at the Computerized Conferencing & Communications Centre, New Jersey Institute of Technology, and funded by the National Science Foundation from 1976–1980.
Entry	In the BLEND system an Entry is a public message to all the members of an Activity and can be likened to making a statement or asking a question at a conference.
FORUM	A computer conferencing suite developed at the Institute of the Future by J. Vallee and colleagues.
HCI	Human-Computer Interaction (see also CHF).
Infomedia	The Infomedia Corporation, Palo Alto, California, supplier of the NOTEPAD software suite as a basis for the BLEND system.
Intelligent VDU	Terminal incorporating a microprocessor and capable of performing fairly simple tasks, e.g. validation, independently of the large computer to which it is connected.
Interactive software	Programs that lead the operator through a series of operations by questions and answers.
IPSS	International Packet Switch Stream.
LINC	Loughborough Information Network Community. The particular community of people involved in the experimental programme of scientific communication with various types of electronic journal, and especially with the electronic journal *Computer Human Factors*.
LUT	Loughborough University of Technology and particularly Department of Human Sciences.

MCC	Man-computer communication (see also CHF).
Menu driven	A program whose execution is controlled by the selection of choices from a list presented on a screen.
Microcomputers	Small, relatively cheap computers powered by microprocessors.
MIDNET	The Midland universities' computer network, connecting Warwick, Aston, Birmingham, Nottingham, Loughborough and Leicester.
Note	In the BLEND system, a Note is a private message from sender to recipient and only visible to them.
NOTEPAD	The name of a software suite which is a proprietary product of the Infomedia Corporation; it is a revised and rewritten version of PLANET. This has been rented by the BL for the .four-year experimental programme and been mounted on the University of Birmingham DEC20 to form the software basis of the BLEND system. Developed from FORUM and PLANET.
OCR	Optical Character Recognition — input to a computer direct from a printed document without the usual intermediate punching stage. The typeface required is often controlled (e.g. OCR-B) and is 'read' by the computer by projecting the image of the character on to a matrix of photocells.
On-line	Direct access from a terminal to a computer's CPU enabling virtually immediate processing of input.
Output	The result of a program run, displayed on a VDU, printer, punched card, paper or magnetic tape.
Password	Short code that must be input before the machine will allow a particular function to be performed.
Peer review	See Refereeing.

PERQ	Brand of computer with sophisticated screen facilities, made by Three Rivers Corporation, USA, and marketed by ICL in Britain.
PLANET	'Planning Network'; a later and simplified version of the FORUM computer conferencing system, subsequently licensed to and marketed by Infomedia Corporation.
PLUTO	An add-on unit to produce high-resolution colour graphics for microcomputers.
Port	Input and output terminations of a CPU to which peripherals may be connected.
Poster Papers	In the BLEND system, papers submitted for 'publication' in the Poster Papers electronic journal, into which they are entered without undergoing the refereeing process and where they are commented upon by readers.
Printer	A peripheral which converts data into hard copy.
Printout	A permanent record (usually on paper) or a data sequence.
Program	A series of instructions executed in a suitable language which, when run on a computer, solves a problem or performs a task.
Project	A Project is a security bounded area of BLEND. To enter a Project a person must have previously been made a member by name and must also use a personal password. Inside each Project there can be many Activities (see Activity).
PSS	Packet Switch Stream — British Telecom's service for packets of information routed from computer to computer, complying with the CCITT Recommendation X25.
PSTN	Public Switched Telephone Network — the national telephone service.

RAAJ

References, Abstracts and Annotations Journal.
Bibliographic reference and authors' abstract
relevant to the interests of Computer Human
Factors.

Refereeing

The evaluation of submitted papers and dispatches
by the editor, associate editors and referees in terms
of their theoretical interest, practical interest,
relevance to Computer Human Factors and read-
ability.

SERCNET

Science and Engineering Research Council computer network, linking the SERC-funded research
institutions, which has recently been renamed
JANET.

Teleconference

Conference carried out at a distance using telecommunications as a medium — includes audio-,
video- and computer teleconferencing.

Telex

System for transmitting at speed written communications internationally.

TORCH

Recommended brand of computer for new installa-
tions considering using the BLEND system.

UNIX

A multi-user, multi-tasking computer proprietary
operating system developed at Bell Laboratories,
USA.

VDU

Visual Display Unit — TV-type screen where data
are displayed.

7 REFERENCES

ALLEN T.J.   1966
Managing the Flow of Scientific and Technological Information.
Unpublished Thesis, Massachusetts Institute of Technology, Cambridge,
Massachusetts.

AMERICAN PSYCHOLOGICAL ASSOCIATION.   1963, 1965,
1969
Reports of Project on Scientific Information Exchange in Psychology.
1 December 1963; 2 December 1965; 3 January 1969.

BACK H.B.   1972
What Information Dissemination Studies Imply Concerning the Design of
On-line Reference Retrieval Systems.
Journal of the American Society for Information Science, 23, 156–163.

BAMFORD H.   1976
A Concept for Applying Computer Technology to the Publication of
Scientific Journals.
Journal of the Washington Academy of Sciences, 62, 306–314.

BENEST I.D. & JONES G.   . 1982
Computer Emulation of Books.
*Proceedings of International Conference on Man-Machine Systems, 6–9 July
1982.* Published by IEE, Conference Publication No. 212.

BERNARD P.   1983
BLEND: a Theoretical and Practical Examination of an Electronic Journal.
Unpublished M.Sc. Thesis, Department of Information Science, City
University.

BLEND PROJECT MANAGEMENT TEAM   1982
Second LINC Community Meeting on 14th December 1981.
Bulletin No. 2, archived in electronic form only in the BLEND system.

BOLT R.A.   1979
Spatial Data Management.
Architecture Machine Group, Massachusetts Institute of Technology,
Cambridge, Massachusetts.

BUCKLEY P.   1983
Optimising Display Terminal Facilities for Elements of the Academic Refereeing Task.
Unpublished M.Sc. Thesis, University College London.

COLE I.   1981
The Role of Human Memory in the External Storage and Retrieval of Information.
Unpublished Ph.D. Thesis, Loughborough University of Technology.

COMMISSION OF THE EUROPEAN COMMUNITIES   1980
The Impact of New Technologies on Publishing.
Proceedings of the symposium held in Luxembourg, 6–7 November, 1979.
London, Munich, New York, Paris: K. G. Saur.

CUFF R.   1980
On Casual Users.
International Journal of Man-Machine Studies, 12(2), 163–189.

DAMODARAN L.   1976
The Role of User Support.
In Shackel B. (Ed.) *Man-Computer Interaction: Human Factors of Computers and People.* Sitjhoff and Noordhof, 1981.

DODD W.P.   1982
Computer Conferencing Aided Learning.
Archived (in electronic form only) in the British Library Research & Development Department Experimental Electronic Journal *Computer Human Factors* CHF1 and to be published in *Computer Education.*

EASON K.D.   1979
Man-computer Communication in Public and Private Computing.
In Shackel B. (Ed.) *Man-Computer Communication Volume 2* Infotech State of the Art Report. Maidenhead: Infotech International.

EASON K.D.   1982
The Process of Introducing Information Technology.
Behaviour and Information Technology, 1(2), 197–213.

EASON K.D., DAMODARAN L. & STEWART T.F.M.   1974
MICA Survey: a Report of a Survey of Man-Computer Interaction in Commercial Applications.
SSRC Project Report on Grant HR 1844/1.

GAINES B.R.   1981
The Technology of Interaction-dialogue Programming Rules.
International Journal of Man-Machine Studies, 14, 133–150.

GIBSON R.   1979
An Annotated Bibliography of Man-computer Communication.
In Shackel B. (Ed.) *Man-Computer Communication*, 1, 301–337 Infotech
State of the Art Report. Maidenhead: Infotech International.

GRINGAS L.   1976
Psychological Self-image of the Systems Analyst.
*Proceedings of 14th Annual Computer and Personnel Research Conference,
Alexandria, USA 29–30 July 1976*, 121–132.

GROGAN D.   1982
Science and Technology. 4th Edition.
London: Clive Bingley.

HARRI-AUGSTEIN S., SMITH M. & THOMAS L.   1982
Reading to Learn.
London, New York: Methuen.

HILLS P., HULL J. & PULLINGER D.   1983
An Experiment on the Redesign of Journal Articles for On-Line Viewing.
Final report to BNB Research Fund, April 1983. HUSAT Memo. No. 275,
BNB RF Report 14, Department of Human Sciences, Loughborough
University of Technology.

HILTZ S.R. & TUROFF M.   1978
The Network Nation: Human Communication via Computer.
Reading, Massachusetts: Addison-Wesley.

JOHANSEN R., VALLEE J., & SPANGLER, K.   1979
Electronic Meetings: Technical Alternatives and Social Choices.
Reading, Massachusetts: Addison-Wesley.

KEENAN S.   1980
Abstracting and Indexing Services.
In Bourne R. (Ed.) *Serials Librarianship.* London: The Library Association.

LANCASTER F.W.   1978
Towards Paperless Information Systems.
New York: Academic Press.

LINE M.   1981
Redesigning Information Packages for Electronic Transmission.
In Jones K.P. and Taylor H. (Eds.) *Design of Information Systems for Human Beings.* London: Aslib.

MAGUIRE M.   1982
Computer Recognition of Textual Keyboard Inputs from Naive Users.
Behaviour and Information Technology, 1(1), 93–111.

MARTYN J.   1964
Report of an Investigation on Literature Searching by Research Scientists.
London: Aslib Research Department.

MAUDE T.I. & DODD W.P.   1983
A Rapid Prototyping Case Study.
Centre for Computing and Computer Studies, University of Birmingham.

MAUDE T.I. & PULLINGER D.J.   1984
Software for Reading, Refereeing and Browsing in the BLEND System.
To be published in *Computer Journal.*

MEADOWS A.J.   1980
New Technology and Developments in the Communication of Research During the 1980s.
Leicester University Primary Communications Research Centre, Occasional Paper, BLR&D Report 5562.

MILLER D.P.   1981
The Depth-breadth Trade-off in Hierarchical Computer Menus.
Proceedings of 25th Annual Conference of Human Factors Society, 296–300.

MILLER L.A. & THOMAS J.C.   1977
Behavioural Issues in the Use of Interactive Systems.
International Journal of Man-Machine Studies, 9, 509–536.

MUTER P., LATREMOUILLE S.A. & TREURNIET W.C.   1982
Extended Reading of Continuous Text on Television Screens.
Human Factors, 24(5), 501–508.

PALME J.   1981
Experience with the Use of the COM Computerized Conferencing System.
FOA Report No. C 10166E-M6(H9). Swedish National Defence Research Institute, 104 50 Stockholm.

PALME J. & ENDERIN L.   1982
COM Teleconferencing System – Concise Manual.
FOA Report No. C10129E-M6(E5). Swedish National Defence Research
Institute, 104 50 Stockholm.

PULLINGER D.J.   1982
*6-Month Phone Survey of the LINC Community on BLEND – a Short
Factual Account.*
HUSAT Memo. No. 258, Department of Human Sciences, Loughborough
University of Technology.

PULLINGER D.J.   1984a
The Analysis of the Editorial Procedure for Refereeing in Two Journals.
In preparation.

PULLINGER D.J.   1984b
Enhancing NOTEPAD Teleconferencing for the BLEND Electronic
Journal.
Behaviour and Information Technology, 3(1), 13–23.

PULLINGER D.J.   1984c
*Thirty-five Month Phone Survey of the LINC Community on BLEND — a
Short Factual Account.*
HUSAT Memo. No. 291, Department of Human Sciences, Loughborough
University of Technology.

PULLINGER D.J., SHACKEL B., DODD W. & MAUDE T.   1982
Questions Answered Relating to the BLEND Electronic Journal
Experimental Programme.
Bulletin of the Association of Learned and Professional Society Publishers,
June 1982.

RAMSEY H.R. & ATWOOD M.E.   1979
Human Factors in Computer Systems: a Review of the Literature.
Office of Naval Research Technical Report SAI-79-111-DEN.

REYNOLDS C.   1983
*An Interactive Database System Designed to Give Terminal Confidence.
An Interactive Paper on Multics.*
Brunel University, Middlesex, UK.

ROYAL SOCIETY   1981
A Study of the Scientific Information System in the United Kingdom.
BLR&D Report 5626, London: Royal Society

SENDERS J.   1977
An On-line Scientific Journal.
The Information Scientist, 11(1), March 1977, 3–9.

SHACKEL B.   1979
Man-Computer Communication.
Infotech State of the Art Report Two volumes. Maidenhead: Infotech
International.

SHACKEL B.   1980
*Visit to USA in April 1980 re: Electronic Journal Project – a Confidential
Report to BLR&DD.*
HUSAT Memo. No. 211R, Department of Human Sciences, Loughborough
University of Technology.

SHACKEL B.   1981a
Plans and Initial Progress with BLEND — an Electronic Network
Communication Experiment.
International Journal of Man-Machine Studies, 17, August 1982, 225–33.

SHACKEL B.   1981b
The Concept of Usability.
Paper for IBM Software and Information Usability Symposium, IBM
Poughkeepsie, New York, 15 September 1981.

SHACKEL B.   1982a
The BLEND System — Programme for the Study of some Electronic
Journals.
Computer Journal, 25(2), 161–168, 1982. *Ergonomics,* 25(4), 269–284, 1982.
Journal of the American Society for Information Science, 34(1), 22–30, 1983.

SHACKEL B.   1982b
*Record of BLEND-LINC Users' Teleconference 1–22 November 1982 on
Ideas for Year 3.*
HUSAT Memo. No. 257, Department of Human Sciences, Loughborough
University of Technology.

SHACKEL B.   1983
LINC Manual — 1983.
Department of Human Sciences, Loughborough University of Technology.

SHACKEL B. & PRESTON J.   1980
BL Experimental Electronic Journals Project. Report of Discussions at 1st Infonet Community Meeting - 31 October 1980.
HUSAT Memo. No. 230, Department of Human Sciences, Loughborough University of Technology.

SHERIDAN T., SENDERS J., MORAY N., STOKLOSA J., GUILLAUME J., & MAKEPEACE D.   1981
Experimentation with a Multi-disciplinary Teleconference and Electronic Journal on Mental Workload.
Unpublished Report to National Science Foundation (Division of Science Information Access Improvement) 320 pp, June 1981.

SLATER M. & FISHER P.   1969
Use made of Technical Libraries.
Aslib Occasional Publication No. 2, London: Aslib.

SPENCE R. & APPERLEY M.   1982
Database Navigation: an Office Environment for the Professional.
Behaviour and Information Technology, 1(1), 43–54.

UHLIG R.P. (Ed.)   1981
Computer Message Systems.
Proceedings of the IFIP TC-6 International Symposium on Computer Message Systems, Ottawa, Canada, 6-8 April. 1981. North-Holland Publishing Co. ISBN 0444852536.

URQUHART D.   1965
Physics Abstracting — Use and Users.
Journal of Documentation, 21(2), 113–121.

VAN NES F.C. & VAN DER HEIJDEN J.   1980
Data Retrieval with Hierarchical or Direct Entry Methods.
Talk Presented to the Ergonomics Society Conference, Nottingham.

WAERN Y. & ROLLENHAGEN C.   1983
Reading Text from Visual Display Units (VDUs).
International Journal of Man-Machine Studies, 18, 441–465.

WOOD D. & BOWER C.   1969
The Use of Social Science Periodical Literature.
Journal of Documentation, 25(2), 108–119.

WOODWARD A.   1976
Editorial Processing Centres: Scope in the United Kingdom.
BLR&D Report 5271, London: British Library.

WOODWARD A.M., YSKA, G. & MARTYN J.   1976
The Applicability of Editorial Processing Centres to UK Scholarly Publishing.
BLR&D Report 5270, London: British Library.

WRIGHT P. & LICKORISH A.   1983
Proof-reading Texts on Screen and Paper.
Behaviour and Information Technology, 2(3), 227–235.

ZALTMAN G.   1968
Scientific Recognition and Communication Behavior in High Energy Physics.
Unpublished Ph.D. Thesis, Johns Hopkins University, Maryland.

8 APPENDICES

Appendix 1: List of HUSAT Memoranda Related to BLEND

211 R   *Visit to USA in April 1980 re: Electronic Journal Project. A Confidential Report to BLR&DD.* Shackel B. 1980.

212 R   *Infomedia's NOTEPAD as the Infrastructure for the BL Electronic Journal Report.* Appendix 3 to HUSAT Memo. No. 211 R. Shackel B. 1980.

230   *BL Experimental Electronic Journals Project. Report of Discussions at 1st Infonet Community Meeting — 31 October 1980.* Shackel B. & Preston J. 1980.

253   *Three Papers on the Plans and Initial Progress with BLEND.* Shackel B. 1981.

254   *Three Papers on the BLEND System.* Pullinger D.J. et al. 1982.

257   *Record of BLEND-LINC Users' Teleconference 1–22 November 1982 on Ideas for Year 3.* Shackel B. 1982.

258   *6-Month Phone Survey of the LINC Community on BLEND — a Short Factual Account.* Pullinger D.J. 1982.

261 R   *Human Communication via Computers: Recent Research Findings. Stockholm 30.8.82-1.9.82. A Confidential Report to BLR&DD.* Pullinger D.J. 1982.

265 R   *Report on the Preliminary Evaluation of the MACE Community.* Olphert W. 1982.

266 R   *BLEND Progress and Some Views Ahead.* Shackel B. 1982.

267 R   *Seminar on Generalised Markup Languages. Amsterdam, December 2–3 1982. A Confidential Report to BLR&DD.* Pullinger D.J. 1982.

268 R   *Proposed Standard for Generalised Markup Languages. A Confidential Report to BLR&DD.* Appendix to HUSAT Memo. No. 267 R. Pullinger D.J. 1982.

269   *Enhancing NOTEPAD Teleconferencing for the BLEND 'Electronic Journal'.* Pullinger D.J. & Maude T.I. 1982.

272   *Report on Third LINC Meeting, December 1982.* Buckland W. & Pullinger D.J. 1982.

275   *An Experiment on the Redesign of Journal Articles for On-line Viewing.* Final Report to the British National Bibliography Research Fund. Hills, P., Hull J. & Pullinger D.J. 1983.

276 R   *The Development of the Reference, Abstract and Annotations Journal (RAAJ) on the BLEND System.* Pullinger D.J. & Howey K. 1983.

278   *Report to the BLR&DD: 10th IATUL Biennial Conference, Essen, 6–10 June 1983. The Future of Serials: Publication, Automation & Management.* Shackel B. 1983.

279   *Attitudes to Traditional Journal Procedure.* Pullinger D.J. 1983.

280   *Reading Electronic Journals On-line.* A paper to the British National Bibliography Research Fund. Pullinger D.J. 1983.

283   *BLEND Seminars 25–26 May 1983. Final Discussion Session — Edited from Tape Recorder.* Shackel B. 1983.

284   *Enhancing NOTEPAD Teleconferencing for the BLEND 'Electronic Journal'.* Pullinger D.J. 1983.

288   *Software for Reading, Refereeing and Browsing in the BLEND System.* Maude T.I. & Pullinger D.J. 1983.

289   *Reading Journal Papers On-line.* Pullinger D.J. 1983.

291   *Thirty-five Month Phone Survey of the LINC Community on BLEND: a Short Factual Account.* Pullinger D.J. 1983.

300 R   *The BLEND System: FERN Strategy Document.* Olphert W. & Pullinger D.J. 1984.

301 R   *The BLEND System: BIOTEC Strategy Document.* Webb T. & Pullinger D.J. 1984.

302   *The Fourth LINC Community Meeting — 20th December 1983.*
       Moulding J. 1984.

303   *Ways of Viewing Costs of Journals: Cost Evaluation of the*
       BLEND Experiment. Singleton A. & Pullinger D.J. 1984.

304   *The Design and Presentation of the Computer Human Factors*
       Journal on BLEND. Pullinger D.J. & Shackel B. 1984.

Appendix 2:   List of BLEND Team Publications

DODD W.P.   1983
Electronic Journal Experiment.
Data Processing, 25(5), June 1983, 34–36.

DODD W.P.   1984
Computer Conferencing Aided Learning.
To be Published in *Computer Education*.

MAUDE T. & PULLINGER D.J.   1983
Software for Reading, Refereeing and Browsing in the BLEND System.
To be Published in *Computer Journal*.

MAUDE T., DODD W.P., PULLINGER D.J., & SHACKEL B.
1982
The BLEND Electronic Journal System.
IUCC Bulletin, 5(1), 22–26.

PULLINGER D.J.   1983
Attitudes to Traditional Journal Procedure.
Electronic Publishing Review, 3(3), September 1983, 213–222.

PULLINGER D.J.   1984
Enhancing NOTEPAD Teleconferencing for the BLEND 'Electronic Journal'.
Behaviour and Information Technology 3(1), 1984, 13–23.

PULLINGER D.J. & HOWEY K.   1984
The Development of the *Reference, Abstract and Annotations Journal (RAAJ)* on the BLEND System.
Journal of Librarianship, 16(1), 19–33.

PULLINGER D.J. & SHACKEL B.   1981
A Research Project on Electronic Journals.
Report on ALPSP/PCRC Seminar on New Publishing Technologies, Ed. M. Katzen.
Association of Learned and Professional Society Publishers/Primary Communications Research Centre.

PULLINGER D.J. & SHACKEL B.   1982
BLEND & LINC — Network Communication to Explore Electronic Journals.
Proceedings of the IEE Conference on Man-Machine Systems, UMIST, 6–9 July 1982.

PULLINGER D.J., SHACKEL B., DODD W. & MAUDE T.   1982
Questions Answered Relating to the BLEND 'Electronic Journal' Experimental Programme.
Bulletin of the Association of Learned and Professional Society Publishers, June 1982.

PULLINGER D.J. & SINGLETON A.   1984
Costing Models for Electronic Journals: Cost Evaluation of the BLEND Experiment.
To be published in *Electronic Publishing Review,* 1984.

SHACKEL B.   1981
Plans and Initial Progress with BLEND — an Electronic Network Communication Experiment.
International Journal of Man-Machine Studies, 17, August 1982, 225–33.

SHACKEL B.   1982
The BLEND System — Programme for the Study of some Electronic Journals.
Computer Journal, 25(2), 1982, 161–168. *Ergonomics,* 25(4), 1982, 269–284. *Journal of the American Society for Information Science,* 34(1), 1983, 22–30.

SHACKEL B.   1982
Are Serials on the Way Out?
Proceedings of UK Serials Group Conference 'The Information Chain' Ed. John A. Urquhart.
Serial Monographs No. 5. London: UK Serials Group.

SHACKEL B., PULLINGER D.J., MAUDE T. & DODD P.   1983
The BLEND-LINC Project on 'Electronic Journals' after Two Years.
Aslib Proceedings, 35(2), February 1982, 77–91. *The Computer Journal,* 26(3), 1983, 247–252.

SINGLETON A. & PULLINGER D.J.   1984
Ways of Viewing Costs of Journals: Cost Evaluation of the BLEND Experiment.
Electronic Publishing Review, 4(1), 59–71.

Appendix 3: List of BLEND Talks

1981

11 February — by Shackel — To the Department of Library and Information Studies — Loughborough University of Technology.

12 February — by Shackel — To the Seminar at PIRA on New Technology — (Printing Industry Research Association).

12 March — by Shackel — To the Primary Communications Research Centre — University of Leicester.

18 March — by Dodd & Maude — To the Computer Centre Seminar Group — University of Birmingham.

3 April — by Shackel — To the Ergonomics Society Annual Conference, University of York.

6 May — by Shackel — To the Seminar on 'New Technology & the Book World' at Banbury, organised by the British National Bibliography Research Fund.

22 July — by Shackel & Pullinger — To the 8th Cranfield Conference on Mechanised Information Transfer, Cranfield.

22 September — by Pullinger — To the Seminar 'New Technologies' organised jointly by the Association of Learned and Professional Society Publishers and the Primary Communications Research Centre.

12-16 October. — by Shackel — To the Annual Conference of the Human Factors Society, Rochester, N.Y.

December — by Shackel, Pullinger, Dodd & Maude — Seminar series organised by the BLR&DD at Novello House.

1982

12 May — by Pullinger — To the Institute of Information Scientists, Midlands Branch Annual General Meeting — Loughborough University of Technology.

13 May — by Pullinger — To the HUSAT Research Group, Loughborough University of Technology.

15 May — by Pullinger — To the course entitled 'Electronic Publishing', organised jointly by Microinfo and NRCd, London.

15 September — by Maude — To the IUCC (Interuniversity Committee on Computing) Colloquium in Reading.

21-24 September — by Shackel & Pullinger — To the Aslib 55th Annual Conference, Manchester.

29 September — by Pullinger — To the Library Technology Study Group, Open University.

1983
4 March — by Pullinger — To the Exchange of Experience Seminar on 'Current Research into Scholarly Communication' — University of Leicester.

9 March — by Pullinger — To the Library Studies Department, Loughborough University of Technology.

31 March — by Pullinger — To the British Library Seminar on 'The Management of Change' — School of Librarianship, Leeds Polytechnic.

17 May — by Pullinger — To the Centre for Computing and Computer Studies Department, University of Birmingham.

24 May — by Shackel — To the Advisory Committee for the Research and Development Department (ACORDD), BLR&DD, London.

25-26 May — by Shackel, Pullinger, Dodd & Maude — To Four Seminars on BLEND, organised by the BLR&DD at Novello House.

15 June — by Pullinger — To the Human-Computer Interface Research Unit, Leicester Polytechnic.

6 July — by Pullinger — To the British National Bibliography Research Fund, British Library.

22 July — by Pullinger — To the Second Seminar on 'Basic Information Research', Cranfield, organised by the BLR&DD.

22 November — by Pullinger — To the Conference on 'The Storage and Retrieval of Integrated Graphics and Text' organised by the British Computer Society.

23 November — by Shackel — To the Seminar organised by the Association of Learned and Professional Society Publishers.

6-8 December — by Shackel — To the On-line Information Meeting, London.

Appendix 4: List of Present Projects and Activities in LINC

Projects   *Activities*
NEWS
   1   Messages
   2   LINC Members & Who's Who
   3   LINC Projects and Activities
   4   Advice & Query Corner
   5   LINC News
   6   Computer Human Factors Qs & As
   7   Teleconference on Mail and Conference System Needs
   8   Chit-Chat
   9   Jim Hartley's Questionnaire

LINC PLANS, PROCEDURES AND PROGRESS
   1   Proposals for Development
   2   LINC Papers Progress
   3   Procedures and Conditions
   4   LINC Members List
   5   LINC Readers List
   6   Progress
   7   Project Plan Papers
   8   B. Shackel. Some Ideas for BLEND-LINC Year 3

LINC AUTHOR WRITING
   1   Advice & Help
   2   Messages to & from Editor

BULLETIN
   1   Bulletin 1: First LINC Meeting, 31 October 1980
   2   Bulletin 2: Second LINC Meeting, 14 December 1981
   3   Bulletin 3: Questions Answered Relating to the BLEND System
   4   Sheffield Biomedical Service References On Man-computer Interaction
   5   Bulletin 4: Technical Aspects in Enhancing NOTEPAD for BLEND
   6   Bulletin 5: 6-Month Phone Survey — a Short Factual Account
   7   LINC News Back Copies 1982-83
   8   Bulletin 5: 6-Month Phone Survey — a Short Factual Account
   9   Bulletin 6: Attitudes to Traditional Journal Procedure
  10   Bulletin 7: Reading Papers On-line

POSTER

COMPUTER HUMAN FACTORS 1

Appendix 5: List of Refereed Papers in CHF

BASON G. & WRIGHT P. A Comparison of Alternative Approaches to Multipurpose Software Design. CHF1.

BROADBENT D.E., FITZGERALD P. & BROADBENT M.H.P. Conscious and Unconscious Judgment in the Control of Complex Systems. CHF2.

DODD W.P. Computer Conferencing Aided Learning: Some Initial Experiences. CHF1.

HARTLEY J. & FRASE L.T. Human and Computer Aids to Writing. CHF2.

MORRISON D.L. & GREEN T.R.G. Adaptive Interface Techniques in Recognising Speech and Similar Inputs. CHF1.

SHACKEL B. The BLEND System — Programme for the Study of Some 'Electronic Journals'. CHF1.

SHACKEL B., PULLINGER D.J., MAUDE T.I. & DODD W.P. The BLEND-LINC Project on 'Electronic Journals' After Two Years. CHF2.

WILSON P. Book Review — Human Factors in Office Automation, W.O. Galitz. CHF1.

Appendix 6: List of Poster Papers

COOMBS M.J. & ALTY J.L. An Application of Sinclair's Discourse Analysis System to the Study of Computer Guidance Interactions.

DODD W.P. 5th International Conference on Software Engineering, San Diego, March 1981 — A Personal View.

DODD W.P., RAMSAY P., AXFORD T.H. & PARKYN D.G. A Prototyping Language for Text Processing Applications.

EASON K.D. An Annotated Bibliography on User Friendly Systems.

EDWARDS E. Review of 'Electronic Mail Systems' by J.A. Welch and P.A. Wilson.

EDWARDS E. REFLIST: A Computer-supported Bibliography.

HARTLEY J., RODGERS A. & TRUEMAN M. Qualifying Verbal Quantifiers.

HOPKIN V.D. Some Human Factors Implications of Expert Systems.

HOPKIN V.D. Automation Induced Problems and Potential Problems in Aviation.

INNOCENT P.R. Educating Computing Professionals to Value Human Factors: Part 1 — Principles.

INNOCENT P.R. Educating Computing Professionals to Value Human Factors: Part 2 — An Example.

MAUDE T.I. A Stand-alone Demonstration of the BLEND System Using a TORCH Microcomputer and Ringmaster Slide Projector.

PEARCE B.G. Ergonomics and the Terminal Junky.

PYLE I.C. Copernicus, Computer Networks and BLEND.

REYNOLDS C.F. Was 'John Smith' a Farmer?

WILSON P.A. Recommendations from a Study of Electronic Mailbox Systems.

WILSON P.A. A Review of 'Human Factors in Office Automation' by W.O. Galitz.

WILSON P.A. Computer Input and Output: a Categorisation of the Applied Human Aspects.

WILSON P.A., MAUDE T.I., MARSHALL C.J. & HEATON N.O. The Active Mailbox — Your On-line Secretary.

WRIGHT P. Skips and Steps in Searching an Index.

YOUNG J. & EDMONDS E. Norms of Interpretation and Man-computer Communication.

Appendix 7: List of Original Researchers Invited to Participate

Director and Editor	Shackel
Joint Editors (envisaged so as to share workload and ensure breadth of coverage)	Being invited

Human Sciences (30)

APU Cambridge	Barnard Wright	Nottingham — Psychology	Smith Henry
Aston	Edwards (Whitfield)	NPL	Bevan (Schofield)
Birkbeck	Ballantine	Oxford	Broadbent (Fitzgerald)
IAM	Hopkin		Yates
Keele	Hartley	P.O. Research	Sime
Loughborough — ICE	Moore (Kirk)	S & APU Sheffield	Fitter (Green)
Loughborough — HUSAT	Eason		Moray
	Pearce (Damodaran) (Porter)	Stirling Sussex	Sutherland Long
Nottingham — SAMMIE	Case (Corlett)	UCL Warwick	Kiss (Annett)

Computing and Information Sciences and Related Areas (23)

Birkbeck	Florentin	NCC	Connor
Birmingham	Lang		Pritchard (Fairbairn) (Coan)
Brunel	Reynolds (Pitteway)	NPL	Davies
DoE PSA	Thompson	Queen Mary College	Thimbleby (Coulouris)
Imperial	Spence (Apperley)	Strathclyde	Maver
Leicester Polytechnic	Innocent (Edmonds)	UCL	Kirstein
Liverpool	Alty (Coombs)	York	Pyle
Loughborough — Computer Studies	Newman (Evans)		

Project Group

Birmingham	Jarratt	BLR&DD	Pinnock
	Dodd		Graddon
	(Schonfelder)		(Gray for
			information)
Loughborough	Shackel		
	Pullinger		

N.B. In the lists of participant members above, the names of principal participants are given first and the names of known associates are given in brackets; named and other associates may enter papers and participate through the 'sponsorship' and connection cost allowance of the principal.

Appendix 8: List of Present Researchers in the LINC

Arnott (John)	University of Dundee
Astley (Bob)	Pilkington Bros.
Atherton (Marc)	University of Aston in Birmingham
Bacsich (Paul)	The Open University
Ballantine (Malcolm)	Birkbeck College
Barber (Derek)	Alvey Directorate
Barnard (Phillip)	MRC Applied Psychology Unit
Bate (John)	Napier College
Begg (Karen)	University College London
Benest (Ian)	SERC Rutherford Appleton Laboratory
Bevan (Nigel)	National Physical Laboratory
Bisseret (Andre)	INRIA
Borwick (Leo)	British Telecom Research Laboratories
Branthwaite (Alan)	University of Keele
Broadbent (Donald)	University of Oxford
Brooks (Andrew)	University of Strathclyde
Brown (Ivan)	MRC Applied Psychology Unit
Browne (Dermott)	Hatfield Polytechnic
Bull (Ken)	Hatfield Polytechnic
Cannon (Terry)	BLR&DD
Case (Keith)	Loughborough University of Technology
Christie (Bruce)	ITT
Clarke (Ann)	BLR&DD
Condon (Maurice)	National Computing Centre
Coombs (Mike)	University of Strathclyde
Coulouris (George)	Queen Mary College
David (Hugh)	Eurocontrol Experimental Centre
Day (Paul)	British Aerospace Dynamics Group
Dodd (Peter)	University of Birmingham
Eason (Ken)	HUSAT, Loughborough University of Technology
Edmonds (Ernest)	Leicester Polytechnic
Edwards (Elwyn)	University of Aston in Birmingham
Fitzgerald (Peter)	University of Oxford
Florentin (John)	Birkbeck College
Fox (John)	Imperial Cancer Research Fund
Gilbert (Nigel)	University of Surrey
Goodman (Tom)	-
Graddon (Pamela)	BLR&DD
Green (Thomas)	MRC Social and Applied Psychology Research Unit

Hale (David)	Queens University
Hammersley (Peter)	Middlesex Polytechnic
Hammond (Nick)	MRC Applied Psychology Unit
Hartley (Jim)	University of Keele
Heaton (Nigel)	GEC Hirst Research Centre
Heller (Leon)	-
Henry (Roger)	University of Nottingham
Herrick (George)	Westland Helicopters Ltd.
Hopkin (David)	R.A.E., Farnborough
Innocent (Peter)	Leicester Polytechnic
Jarratt (Peter)	University of Birmingham
Jonassen (David)	Visiting University of Keele
Jones (Peter)	University of Essex
Kaplan (Michael)	Institute for Behavioural Science, US Army Research Establishment
Kirstein (Peter)	University College London
Kiss (George)	University of Warwick
Kornbrot (Diana)	Hatfield Polytechnic
Life (Martin)	British Aerospace Dynamics Group
Line (Maurice)	British Library Lending Division
Lloyd (Elizabeth)	University of Birmingham
Long (John)	University College London
Marshall (Chris)	GEC Hirst Research Centre
Maude (Tim)	University of Birmingham
Maver (Tom)	University of Strathclyde
Monk (Andrew)	University of York
Moulding (Jackie)	HUSAT, Loughborough University of Technology
Murray (Dianne)	National Physical Laboratory
Newell (Alan)	University of Dundee
Newman (Ian)	Loughborough University of Technology
Olphert (Wendy)	HUSAT, Loughborough University of Technology
Payne (Stephen)	MRC Social and Applied Psychology Research Unit
Pearce (Brian)	HUSAT, Loughborough University of Technology
Pickering (Adrian)	University of Dundee
Pritchard (John)	National Computer Centre
Pullinger (David)	HUSAT, Loughborough University of Technology
Pyle (Ian)	University of York
Reynolds (Chris)	Brunel University
Rubin (Tony)	British Telecom Research Laboratories
Rydz (Andrew)	British Aerospace Dynamics Group
Sandelin (Jon)	University of Stanford
Shackel (Brian)	Loughborough University of Technology
Smith (Hugh)	University of Nottingham

Southall (Richard)	University of Reading
Spence (Robert)	Imperial College of Science and Technology
Stewart (Tom)	Systems Concepts Ltd.
Stone (Bob)	British Aerospace Dynamics Group
Tagg (Stephen)	University of Strathclyde
Thompson (Brian)	Radioactive Waste
Webb (Terry)	HUSAT, Loughborough University of Technology
Wellavize (Dawn)	HUSAT, Loughborough University of Technology
Whitehead (Edward)	Kingston Polytechnic
Whitfield (David)	University of Aston in Birmingham
Williams (Phil)	UMIST
Wilson (Paul)	National Computer Centre
Wright (Pat)	MRC Applied Psychology Unit
Yates (Roy)	British Telecom
Young (Richard)	MRC Applied Psychology Unit

OTHER REPORTS

Library and Information Research (LIR) Reports may be purchased from Publications Sales Unit, British Library Lending Division, Boston Spa, Wetherby, West Yorkshire LS23 7BQ, UK. Prices are available on application. Details of some other LIR Reports are given below.

LIR Report 19. Collier, M. *Local area networks: the implications for library and information science.* February 1984. pp viii + 45. ISBN 0 7123 3028 3. Local area networks are systems allowing high-speed interconnection of computers within a restricted area. They facilitate distributed processing and indicate a trend away from large, centralised computers. Micro-computer networks are being offered as alternatives to minicomputers for substantial data-processing activities. This report, commissioned in 1982, gives definitions, describes concepts and introduces some of the techniques involved. The role of local area networks in library and information science is examined, current initiatives are reviewed and finally some suggestions are made for further research in the field.

LIR Report 20. Flowerdew, A D J, Oldman C M and Whitehead, C M E. *The pricing and provision of information: some recent official reports.* August 1984. pp viii + 96. ISBN 0 7123 3029 1.
The purpose of this report is to examine the economic principles relevant to the issues raised in some recent reports considering the production and dissemination of information in electronic form. It also seeks to compare these principles with those stated or implied in the text of the reports and to draw any justifiable policy conclusions. Since the production and dissemination of information have some characteristics which resemble those of the production and dissemination of ordinary economic goods and services, some which resemble more closely those of other types of economic activity such as transport, and some features which can be considered unique, the authors examine whether this was being taken into account in these reports. They also try to establish whether new theoretical results were being used or new empirical evidence cited, which would have implications elsewhere.

LIR Report 21. Stephens, J. *Inventory of abstracting and indexing services produced in the UK.* October 1983. pp viii + 220. ISBN 0 7123 3030 5. This inventory updates BLR&D Report 5420 of the same title. The entries are arranged alphabetically by name of service. Four indexes are provided: broad subject headings, specific subject headings, an index of responsible authorities, and an index of database processors with the UK online databases they offer.

LIR Report 23. *Information demand and supply in British industry 1977-1983.* October 1983. pp xxii + 118. ISBN 0 7123 3033 X.
Between November 1982 and April 1983 a study was conducted into the effects of the current recession on the supply of technical and commercial information services in British industry. The purpose was to see how industrial information services have adjusted and to investigate how information providers outside industry have reacted to any changes in demand from industry. Questionnaires were distributed among 238 library and information service units in industry, and among 305 external information providers of various kinds. More than half of these provided responses that were analysed. There is evidence that the pattern of demand for, and supply of, information in British industry has changed substantially, and possibly permanently, since 1977.

LIR Report 24. Rudduck, J and Hopkins, D. *The sixth form and libraries: problems of access to knowledge.* July 1984. pp xii + 126. ISBN 0 7123 3034 8.
The concerns of the project can be summarised in a statement by its director:

> It is about the transition of pupils to studentship ... moves from dependence on instruction to capacity for independent study — that kind of move depends on a change in the epistemology of the learner ... there must be a point when the person discovers something of the problematic nature of knowledge. Most people don't do that lower down [the school].

The project was designed as a multi-site case study programme involving teachers, students and librarians in 24 institutions covering a range of sixth form settings. The selection of institutions took account of the need to have access to different environmental and social settings and different levels of library provision. Interviews were the main method of data gathering, and they focused on a core of interrelated topics: academic study in the sixth form, pedagogy, books, libraries and the idea of independent learning.

LIR Report 25. Ratcliffe, F W with the assistance of Patterson, D. *Preservation policies and conservation in British libraries: report of the Cambridge University Library Conservation Project.* February 1984. pp xii + 134. ISBN 0 7123 3035 6.
The Cambridge Conservation Project had two immediate objectives: to establish the facts about preservation policies and practices in libraries in the UK and to identify the educational and training facilities available to librarians and practitioners. Nationwide surveys by questionnaires, interviews and seminars were among the methods used. The report makes recommendations for action in two areas, first within individual libraries, involving little or no additional expenditure and immediately applicable,

secondly at a national level. Among the latter, the twin needs for co-operative action, for which no mechanism exists at present, and for a focal point for preservation, some sort of National Advisory and Research Centre, are of prime importance. The status, funding and location of the latter need further clarification but involvement of the British Library in any such undertaking seems essential to its success.

LIR Report 26. Teskey, F N. *Information retrieval systems for the future.* October 1984. pp viii + 72. ISBN 0 7123 3037 2.
In the first part of the report, the author describes those functions of free-text information systems regarded as fundamental by a number of users. He then goes on to look at some existing and proposed hardware and software methods for implementing such systems. Finally, he proposes a design for a new information retrieval system. Methods of implementing such a system are discussed and some possible applications are outlined.

LIR Report 27. Barrett, R. *Further developments in optical disc technology and applications.* July 1984. pp viii + 34. ISBN 0 7123 3038 0.

During a visit to the USA in April 1983, the author updated information on current developments in optical disc technology and applications. He looked at developments in both the optical video disc and the digital optical recording disc. The data presented in the report are based on information given in the form of discussions and technical papers by staff of the Library of Congress, the National Library of Medicine and BRS Medical.

LIR Report 28. Templeton, R and Witten, A. *Study of cataloguing computer software: applying* AACR2 *to microcomputer programs.* August 1984. pp viii + 77. ISBN 0 7123 3041 0.
Using education as an example, this project established and tested some guidelines for the cataloguing of microcomputer software, based on an examination of Chapter 9 of *AACR2.* Over 200 programs were catalogued, in three stages, two interpretive and one of application. The results of the project include recommendations for bibliographic control, including guidelines for publishers, and for cataloguing standards, and a brief manual of practice for cataloguers.